Division for Ocean Affairs and the Law of
Office of Legal Affairs

Law *of* the Sea

Bulletin No. 80

United Nations
New York, 2013

NOTE

The designations employed and the presentation of the material in this publication do not imply the expression of any opinion whatsoever on the part of the Secretariat of the United Nations concerning the legal status of any country, territory, city or area or of its authorities, or concerning the delimitation of its frontiers or boundaries.

Furthermore, publication in the *Bulletin* of information concerning developments relating to the law of the sea emanating from actions and decisions taken by States does not imply recognition by the United Nations of the validity of the actions and decisions in question.

IF ANY MATERIAL CONTAINED IN THE *BULLETIN* IS REPRODUCED IN PART OR IN WHOLE, DUE ACKNOWLEDGEMENT SHOULD BE GIVEN.

CONTENTS (continued)

CONTENTS (continued)

I. UNITED NATIONS CONVENTION ON THE LAW OF THE SEA

Status of the United Nations Convention on the Law of the Sea, of the Agreement relating to the Implementation of Part XI of the Convention and of the Agreement for the Implementation of the Provisions of the Convention relating to the Conservation and Management of Straddling Fish Stocks and Highly Migratory Fish Stocks [1]

1. Table recapitulating the status of the Convention and of the related Agreements, as at 30 November 2012

This consolidated table, prepared by the Division for Ocean Affairs and the Law of the Sea, Office of the Legal Affairs, provides unofficial, quick reference information related to the participation in UNCLOS and the two implementing Agreements. For official information on the status of these treaties, please refer to the publication entitled "*Multilateral Treaties deposited with the Secretary-General*" (http://untreaty.un.org). The symbol "☐" indicates (i) that a declaration or statement was made at the time of signature; at the time of ratification/accession or anytime thereafter, or (ii) declarations confirmed upon succession. A double icon (☐☐) indicates that two declarations were made by the State. The abbreviation (fc) indicates a formal confirmation; (a) an accession; (s) a succession; (ds) a definitive signature; (p) the consent to be bound; (sp) a simplified procedure. Names of States in *italics* indicate non-members of the United Nations; shaded rows indicate landlocked States.

State or entity	UNCLOS (in force as from 16/11/1994)			Agreement on Part XI (in force as from 28/07/1996)			UN Fish Stocks Agreement (in force as from 11/12/2001)		
	Signature dd/mm/yy	Ratification/ accession; dd/mm/yy	Declaration	Signature dd/mm/yy	Ratification/ accession; dd/mm/yy	Declaration	Signature dd/mm/yy	Ratification/ accession; dd/mm/yy	Declaration
TOTALS	157	164		79	143		59	80	
Afghanistan	18/03/83								
Albania		23/06/03(a)			23/06/03(p)				
Algeria	10/12/82 ☐	11/06/96	☐	29/07/94	11/06/96(p)				
Andorra									
Angola	10/12/82 ☐	05/12/90	☐		07/09/2010(p)				
Antigua and Barbuda	07/02/83	02/02/89							
Argentina	05/10/84 ☐	01/12/95	☐	29/07/94	01/12/95		04/12/95		
Armenia		09/12/02(a)			09/12/02(a)				
Australia	10/12/82	05/10/94	☐	29/07/94	05/10/94		04/12/95	23/12/99	
Austria	10/12/82	14/07/95	☐	29/07/94	14/07/95		27/06/96	19/12/03	☐
Azerbaijan									

[1] Source: Chapter XXI.6 of the publication entitled "*Multilateral Treaties Deposited with the Secretary-General*" at http://treaties.un.org/.

State or entity	UNCLOS (in force as from 16/11/1994)			Agreement on Part XI (in force as from 28/07/1996)		UN Fish Stocks Agreement (in force as from 11/12/2001)		
	Signature dd/mm/yy	Ratification/ accession; dd/mm/yy	Declaration	Signature dd/mm/yy	Ratification/ accession; dd/mm/yy	Signature dd/mm/yy	Ratification/ accession; dd/mm/yy	Declaration
Bahamas	10/12/82	29/07/83		29/07/94	28/07/95(sp)		16/01/97(a)	
Bahrain	10/12/82	30/05/85						
Bangladesh	10/12/82	27/07/01	□□		27/07/01(a)	04/12/95	05/11/12	
Barbados	10/12/82	12/10/93		15/11/94	28/07/95(sp)		22/09/00(a)	
Belarus	10/12/82□	30/08/06	□		30/08/06(a)			
Belgium	05/12/84□	13/11/98	□	29/07/94	13/11/98(p)	03/10/96	19/12/03	□
Belize	10/12/82	13/08/83			21/10/94(ds)	04/12/95	14/07/05	
Benin	30/08/83	16/10/97			16/10/97(p)			
Bhutan	10/12/82							
Bolivia (Plurinational State of)	27/11/84□	28/04/95			28/04/95(p)			
Bosnia and Herzegovina		12/01/94(s)						
Botswana	05/12/84	02/05/90			31/01/05(a)			
Brazil	10/12/82□	22/12/88	□	29/07/94	25/10/07	04/12/95	08/03/00	
Brunei Darussalam	05/12/84	05/11/96			05/11/96(p)			
Bulgaria	10/12/82	15/05/96			15/05/96(a)		13/12/06(a)	□
Burkina Faso	10/12/82	25/01/05		30/11/94	25/01/05(p)	15/10/96		
Burundi	10/12/82							
Cambodia	01/07/83							
Cameroon	10/12/82	19/11/85		24/05/95	28/08/02			
Canada	10/12/82	07/11/03	□	29/07/94	07/11/03	04/12/95	03/08/99	□
Cape Verde	10/12/82□	10/08/87	□	29/07/94	23/04/08			
Central African Republic	04/12/84							
Chad	10/12/82	14/08/09			14/08/09(p)			
Chile	10/12/82□	25/08/97	□		25/08/97(a)			
China	10/12/82	07/06/96	□□	29/07/94	07/06/96(p)	06/11/96□		
Colombia	10/12/82							
Comoros	06/12/84	21/06/94						
Congo	10/12/82	09/07/08			09/07/08(p)			

State or entity	UNCLOS (in force as from 16/11/1994)			Agreement on Part XI (in force as from 28/07/1996)		UN Fish Stocks Agreement (in force as from 11/12/2001)		
	Signature dd/mm/yy	Ratification/ accession; dd/mm/yy	Declaration	Signature dd/mm/yy	Ratification/ accession; dd/mm/yy	Signature dd/mm/yy	Ratification/ accession; dd/mm/yy	Declaration
Cook Islands	10/12/82	15/02/95			15/02/95(a)		01/04/99(a)	
Costa Rica	10/12/82⬜	21/09/92			20/09/01(a)		18/06/01(a)	
Côte d'Ivoire	10/12/82	26/03/84		25/11/94	28/07/95(sp)	24/01/96		
Croatia	10/12/82(s)	05/04/95(s)	⬜		05/04/95(p)			
Cuba	10/12/82⬜	15/08/84	⬜		17/10/02(a)			
Cyprus	10/12/82	12/12/88		01/11/94	27/07/95		25/09/02(a)	
Czech Republic	22/02/93	21/06/96	⬜	16/11/94	21/06/96		19/03/07(a)	⬜
Democratic People's Republic of Korea	10/12/82							
Democratic Republic of the Congo	22/08/83	17/02/89						
Denmark	10/12/82	16/11/04	⬜	29/07/94	16/11/04	27/06/96	19/12/03	⬜
Djibouti	10/12/82	08/10/91						
Dominica	28/03/83	24/10/91						
Dominican Republic	10/12/82	10/07/09	⬜		10/07/09(p)			
Ecuador		24/09/12(a)	⬜		24/09/12(p)			
Egypt	10/12/82	26/08/83	⬜	22/03/95		05/12/95		
El Salvador	05/12/84							
Equatorial Guinea	30/01/84	21/07/97	⬜		21/07/97(p)			
Eritrea			⬜					
Estonia		26/08/05(a)	⬜		26/08/05(a)		07/08/06(a)	⬜
Ethiopia	10/12/82							
European Union	07/12/84⬜	01/04/98(fc)	⬜	29/07/94	01/04/98(fc)	27/06/96⬜	19/12/03	⬜
Fiji	10/12/82	10/12/82	⬜	29/07/94	28/07/95	04/12/95	12/12/96	⬜
Finland	10/12/82⬜	21/06/96	⬜	29/07/94	21/06/96	27/06/96	19/12/03	⬜
France	10/12/82⬜	11/04/96	⬜	29/07/94	11/04/96	04/12/96⬜	19/12/03	⬜
Gabon	10/12/82	11/03/98	⬜	04/04/95	11/03/98(p)	07/10/96		
Gambia	10/12/82	22/05/84						
Georgia		21/03/96(a)			21/03/96(p)			
Germany		14/10/94(a)	⬜	29/07/94	14/10/94	28/08/96	19/12/03	⬜
Ghana	10/12/82	7/06/83	⬜					

State or entity	UNCLOS (in force as from 16/11/1994) Signature dd/mm/yy	Ratification/accession; dd/mm/yy	Declaration	Agreement on Part XI (in force as from 28/07/1996) Signature dd/mm/yy	Ratification/accession; dd/mm/yy	UN Fish Stocks Agreement (in force as from 11/12/2001) Signature dd/mm/yy	Ratification/accession; dd/mm/yy	Declaration
Greece	10/12/82	21/07/95	▯	29/07/94	21/07/95	27/06/96	19/12/03	▯
Grenada	10/12/82	25/04/91		14/11/94	28/07/95(sp)			
Guatemala	08/07/83	11/02/97	▯		11/02/97(p)			
Guinea	04/10/84	06/09/85	▯	26/08/94	28/07/95(sp)		16/09/05(a)	
Guinea-Bissau	10/12/82	25/08/86			25/09/08(a)	04/12/95		
Guyana	10/12/82	16/11/93						
Haiti	10/12/82	31/07/96			31/07/96(p)			
Holy See								
Honduras	10/12/82	05/10/93	▯		28/07/03(a)		16/05/08(a)	▯
Hungary	10/12/82	05/02/02	▯		05/02/02(a)			
Iceland	10/12/82	21/06/85	▯	29/07/94	28/07/95(sp)	04/12/95	14/02/97	▯
India	10/12/82	29/06/95	▯	29/07/94	29/06/95		19/08/03(a)	
Indonesia	10/12/82	03/02/86		29/07/94	02/06/00	04/12/95	28/09/09	
Iran (Islamic Republic of)	10/12/82						17/04/98(a)	
Iraq	10/12/82	30/07/85						
Ireland	10/12/82	21/06/96	▯	29/07/94	21/06/96	27/06/96	19/12/03	▯
Israel			▯▯	04/12/95				
Italy	07/12/84	13/01/95	▯	29/07/94	13/01/95	27/06/96	19/12/03	▯
Jamaica	10/12/82	21/03/83		29/07/94	28/07/95(sp)	04/12/95		
Japan	07/02/83	20/06/96		29/07/94	20/06/96	19/11/96	07/08/06	
Jordan		27/11/95(a)			27/11/95(p)			
Kazakhstan								
Kenya	10/12/82	02/03/89			29/07/94(ds)		13/07/04(a)	
Kiribati		24/02/03(a)	▯		24/02/03(p)		15/09/05(a)	
Kuwait	10/12/82	02/05/86	▯		02/08/02(a)			
Kyrgyzstan								
Lao People's Democratic Republic	10/12/82	05/06/98		27/10/94	05/06/98(p)			
Latvia		23/12/04(a)	▯		23/12/04(a)		05/02/07(a)	▯
Lebanon	07/12/84	05/01/95			05/01/95(p)			

State or entity	UNCLOS (in force as from 16/11/1994)			Agreement on Part XI (in force as from 28/07/1996)		UN Fish Stocks Agreement (in force as from 11/12/2001)		
	Signature dd/mm/yy	Ratification/ accession; dd/mm/yy	Declaration	Signature dd/mm/yy	Ratification/ accession; dd/mm/yy	Signature dd/mm/yy	Ratification/ accession; dd/mm/yy	Declaration
Lesotho	10/12/82	31/05/07			31/05/07(p)			
Liberia	10/12/82	25/09/08			25/09/08(p)		16/09/05(a)	
Libya	03/12/84							
Liechtenstein	30/11/84							
Lithuania		12/11/03(a)	☐		12/11/03(a)		01/03/07(a)	☐
Luxembourg	05/12/84☐	05/10/00		29/07/94	05/10/00	27/06/96	19/12/03	☐
Madagascar	25/02/83	22/08/01			22/08/01(p)			
Malawi	07/12/84	28/09/10			28/09/10(p)			
Malaysia	10/12/82	14/10/96	☐	02/08/94	14/10/96(p)			
Maldives	10/12/82	07/09/00		10/10/94	07/09/00(p)	08/10/96	30/12/98	
Mali	19/10/83☐	16/07/85						
Malta	10/12/82	20/05/93	☐	29/07/94	26/06/96		11/11/01(a)	☐
Marshall Islands		09/08/91(a)				04/12/95	19/03/03	
Mauritania	10/12/82	17/07/96		02/08/94	17/07/96(p)	21/12/95		
Mauritius	10/12/82	04/11/94			04/11/94(p)		25/03/97(a)	☐
Mexico	10/12/82	18/03/83	☐		10/04/03(a)			
Micronesia (Federated States of)		29/04/91(a)		10/08/94	06/09/95	04/12/95	23/05/97	
Monaco	10/12/82	20/03/96		30/11/94	20/03/96(p)		09/06/99(a)	
Mongolia	10/12/82	13/08/96		17/08/94	13/08/96(p)			
Montenegro		23/10/06(d)	☐		23/10/06(d)			
Morocco	10/12/82	31/05/07	☐	19/10/94	31/05/07	04/12/95	19/09/2012	
Mozambique	10/12/82	13/03/97			13/03/97(a)		10/12/08(a)	
Myanmar	10/12/82	21/05/96			21/05/96(a)			
Namibia	10/12/82	18/04/83		29/07/94	28/07/95(sp)	19/04/96	08/04/98	
Nauru	10/12/82	23/01/96			23/01/96(p)		10/01/97(a)	
Nepal	10/12/82	02/11/98			02/11/98(p)			
Netherlands	10/12/82	28/06/96	☐	29/07/94	28/06/96	28/06/96☐	19/12/03	☐
New Zealand	10/12/82	19/07/96		29/07/94	19/07/96	04/12/95	19/12/03	
Nicaragua	09/12/84☐	03/05/00	☐		03/05/00(p)		18/04/01	

State or entity	UNCLOS (in force as from 16/11/1994) Signature dd/mm/yy	UNCLOS Ratification/accession dd/mm/yy	UNCLOS Declaration	Agreement on Part XI (in force as from 28/07/1996) Signature dd/mm/yy	Agreement on Part XI Ratification/accession dd/mm/yy	UN Fish Stocks Agreement (in force as from 11/12/2001) Signature dd/mm/yy	UN Fish Stocks Agreement Ratification/accession dd/mm/yy	Declaration
Niger	10/12/82							
Nigeria	10/12/82	14/08/86		25/10/94	28/07/95(sp)		02/11/09(a)	
Niue	05/12/84	11/10/06	□		11/10/06(p)	04/12/95	11/10/06	□
Norway	10/12/82	24/06/96	□		24/06/96(a)	04/12/95	30/12/96	
Oman	01/07/83 □	17/08/89	□		26/02/97(a)		14/05/08(a)	
Pakistan	10/12/82	26/02/97	□	10/08/94	26/02/97(p)	15/02/96		
Palau		30/09/96(a)	□		30/09/96(p)		26/03/08(a)	
Panama	10/12/82	01/07/96	□		01/07/96(p)		16/12/08(a)	
Papua New Guinea	10/12/82	14/01/97			14/01/97(p)	04/12/95	04/06/99	
Paraguay	10/12/82	26/09/86		29/07/94	10/07/95			
Peru								
Philippines	10/12/82 □	08/05/84	□	15/11/94	23/07/97	30/08/96		
Poland	10/12/82	13/11/98		29/07/94	13/11/98(p)		14/03/06(a)	□
Portugal	10/12/82	03/11/97	□	29/07/94	03/11/97	27/06/96	19/12/03	□
Qatar	27/11/84 □	09/12/02	□		09/12/02(p)		01/02/08	
Republic of Korea	14/03/83	29/01/96	□	07/11/94	29/01/96	26/11/96		
Republic of Moldova		06/02/07(a)	□		06/02/07(p)			
Romania	10/12/82 □	17/12/96	□		17/12/96(a)		16/07/07(a)	
Russian Federation	10/12/82 □	12/03/97	□		12/03/97(a)	04/12/95	04/08/97	□
Rwanda	10/12/82							
Saint Kitts and Nevis	07/12/84	07/01/93						
Saint Lucia	10/12/82	27/03/85				12/12/95	09/08/96	
Saint Vincent and the Grenadines	10/12/82	01/10/93	□				29/10/10(a)	
Samoa	28/09/84	14/08/95		07/07/95	14/08/95(p)	04/12/95	25/10/96	
San Marino								
Sao Tome and Principe	13/07/83 □	03/11/87						
Saudi Arabia	07/12/84	24/04/96	□		24/04/96(p)			
Senegal	10/12/82	25/10/84		09/08/94	25/07/95	04/12/95	30/01/97	

State or entity	UNCLOS (in force as from 16/11/1994)			Agreement on Part XI (in force as from 28/07/1996)		UN Fish Stocks Agreement (in force as from 11/12/2001)		
	Signature dd/mm/yy [2]	Ratification/ accession; dd/mm/yy	Declaration	Signature dd/mm/yy	Ratification/ accession; dd/mm/yy [1]	Signature dd/mm/yy	Ratification/ accession; dd/mm/yy	Declaration
Serbia		12/03/01(s)	□	12/05/95	28/07/95(sp)			
Seychelles	10/12/82	16/09/91		29/07/94	15/12/94	04/12/96	20/03/98	
Sierra Leone	10/12/82	12/12/94			12/12/94(p)			
Singapore	10/12/82	17/11/94			17/11/94(p)			
Slovakia	28/05/93	08/05/96		14/11/94	08/05/96		06/11/08(a)	□
Slovenia		16/06/95(s)	□ □	19/01/95	16/06/95		15/06/06(a)	□
Solomon Islands	10/12/82	23/06/97			23/06/97(p)		13/02/97(a)	
Somalia	10/12/82	24/07/89						
South Africa	05/12/84	23/12/97	□	03/10/94	23/12/97		14/08/03(a)	
South Sudan								
Spain	04/12/84 □	15/01/97	□ □	29/07/94	15/01/97	03/12/96	19/12/03	□
Sri Lanka	10/12/82	19/07/94		29/07/94	28/07/95(sp)	09/10/96	24/10/96	
Sudan	10/12/82 □	23/01/85		29/07/94				
Suriname	10/12/82	09/07/98			09/07/98(p)			
Swaziland	18/01/84	24/09/12		12/10/94	24/09/12(p)			
Sweden	10/12/82 □	25/06/96	□	29/07/94	25/06/96	27/06/96	19/12/03	□
Switzerland	17/10/84	01/05/09	□	26/10/94	01/05/09			
Syrian Arab Republic								
Tajikistan								
Thailand	10/12/82	15/05/11	□		15/05/11(a)			
The former Yugoslav Republic of Macedonia		19/08/94 (s)			19/08/94(p)			
Timor-Leste								
Togo	10/12/82	16/04/85		03/08/94	28/07/95(sp)			
Tonga		02/08/95(a)			2/08/95(p)	04/12/95	31/07/96	
Trinidad and Tobago	10/12/82	25/04/86	□ □	10/10/94	28/07/95(sp)		13/09/06(a)	

2 For further details, see Chapter XXI of the publication entitled "*Multilateral Treaties deposited with the Secretary-General*" (http://untreaty.un.org/ENGLISH/bible/englishinternetbible/partI/chapterXXI/chapterXXI.asp).

State or entity	UNCLOS (in force as from 16/11/1994)			Agreement on Part XI (in force as from 28/07/1996)		UN Fish Stocks Agreement (in force as from 11/12/2001)		
	Signature dd/mm/yy	Ratification/ accession; dd/mm/yy	Declaration	Signature dd/mm/yy	Ratification/ accession; dd/mm/yy	Signature dd/mm/yy	Ratification/ accession; dd/mm/yy	Declaration
Tunisia	10/12/82	24/04/85	☐☐	15/05/95	24/05/02			
Turkey								
Turkmenistan								
Tuvalu	10/12/82	09/12/02			09/12/02(p)		02/02/09(a)	
Uganda	10/12/82	09/11/90		09/08/94	28/07/95(sp)	10/10/96		
Ukraine	10/12/82 ☐	26/07/99	☐	28/02/95	26/07/99	04/12/95	27/02/03	
United Arab Emirates	10/12/82							
United Kingdom		25/07/97(a)	☐☐	29/07/94	25/07/97	04/12/95	10/12/01 19/12/03[2]	☐☐
United Republic of Tanzania	10/12/82	30/09/85	☐	07/10/94	25/06/98	04/12/95		
United States of America				29/07/94			21/08/96	☐
Uruguay	10/12/82 ☐	10/12/92	☐	29/07/94	07/08/07	16/01/96 ☐	10/09/99	☐
Uzbekistan								
Vanuatu	10/12/82	10/08/99		29/07/94	10/08/99(p)	23/07/96		
Venezuela (Bolivarian Republic of)								
Viet Nam	10/12/82	25/07/94	☐		27/04/06(a)			
Yemen	10/12/82 ☐	21/07/87	☐					
Zambia	10/12/82	07/03/83		13/10/94	28/07/95(sp)			
Zimbabwe	10/12/82	24/02/93		28/10/94	28/07/95(sp)			
TOTALS	157	164		79	143	59	80	

2. <u>Chronological lists of ratifications of, accessions and successions to the Convention and the related Agreements, as at 30 November 2012</u>

a.   The Convention

1.   Fiji (10 December 1982)
2.   Zambia (7 March 1983)
3.   Mexico (18 March 1983)
4.   Jamaica (21 March 1983)
5.   Namibia (18 April 1983)
6.   Ghana (7 June 1983)
7.   Bahamas (29 July 1983)
8.   Belize (13 August 1983)
9.   Egypt (26 August 1983)
10.   Côte d'Ivoire (26 March 1984)
11.   Philippines (8 May 1984)
12.   Gambia (22 May 1984)
13.   Cuba (15 August 1984)
14.   Senegal (25 October 1984)
15.   Sudan (23 January 1985)
16.   Saint Lucia (27 March 1985)
17.   Togo (16 April 1985)
18.   Tunisia (24 April 1985)
19.   Bahrain (30 May 1985)
20.   Iceland (21 June 1985)
21.   Mali (16 July 1985)
22.   Iraq (30 July 1985)
23.   Guinea (6 September 1985)
24.   United Republic of Tanzania
        (30 September 1985)
25.   Cameroon (19 November 1985)
26.   Indonesia (3 February 1986)
27.   Trinidad and Tobago (25 April 1986)
28.   Kuwait (2 May 1986)
29.   Nigeria (14 August 1986)
30.   Guinea-Bissau (25 August 1986)
31.   Paraguay (26 September 1986)
32.   Yemen (21 July 1987)
33.   Cape Verde (10 August 1987)
34.   São Tomé and Príncipe
        (3 November 1987)
35.   Cyprus (12 December 1988)
36.   Brazil (22 December 1988)
37.   Antigua and Barbuda (2 February 1989)
38.   Democratic Republic of the Congo
        (17 February 1989)
39.   Kenya (2 March 1989)
40.   Somalia (24 July 1989)
41.   Oman (17 August 1989)
42.   Botswana (2 May 1990)
43.   Uganda (9 November 1990)
44.   Angola (5 December 1990)
45.   Grenada (25 April 1991)

46.   Micronesia (Federated States of)
        (29 April 1991)
47.   Marshall Islands (9 August 1991)
48.   Seychelles (16 September 1991)
49.   Djibouti (8 October 1991)
50.   Dominica (24 October 1991)
51.   Costa Rica (21 September 1992)
52.   Uruguay (10 December 1992)
53.   Saint Kitts and Nevis (7 January 1993)
54.   Zimbabwe (24 February 1993)
55.   Malta (20 May 1993)
56.   Saint Vincent and the Grenadines
        (1 October 1993)
57.   Honduras (5 October 1993)
58.   Barbados (12 October 1993)
59.   Guyana (16 November 1993)
60.   Bosnia and Herzegovina
        (12 January 1994)
61.   Comoros (21 June 1994)
62.   Sri Lanka (19 July 1994)
63.   Viet Nam (25 July 1994)
64.   The former Yugoslav Republic of Macedonia
        (19 August 1994)
65.   Australia (5 October 1994)
66.   Germany (14 October 1994)
67.   Mauritius (4 November 1994)
68.   Singapore (17 November 1994)
69.   Sierra Leone (12 December 1994)
70.   Lebanon (5 January 1995)
71.   Italy (13 January 1995)
72.   Cook Islands (15 February 1995)
73.   Croatia (5 April 1995)
74.   Bolivia (Plurinational State of)
        (28 April 1995)
75.   Slovenia (16 June 1995)
76.   India (29 June 1995)
77.   Austria (14 July 1995)
78.   Greece (21 July 1995)
79.   Tonga (2 August 1995)
80.   Samoa (14 August 1995)
81.   Jordan (27 November 1995)
82.   Argentina (1 December 1995)
83.   Nauru (23 January 1996)
84.   Republic of Korea (29 January 1996)
85.   Monaco (20 March 1996)
86.   Georgia (21 March 1996)
87.   France (11 April 1996)
88.   Saudi Arabia (24 April 1996)
89.   Slovakia (8 May 1996)

90. Bulgaria (15 May 1996)
91. Myanmar (21 May 1996)
92. China (7 June 1996)
93. Algeria (11 June 1996)
94. Japan (20 June 1996)
95. Czech Republic (21 June 1996)
96. Finland (21 June 1996)
97. Ireland (21 June 1996)
98. Norway (24 June 1996)
99. Sweden (25 June 1996)
100. Netherlands (28 June 1996)
101. Panama (1 July 1996)
102. Mauritania (17 July 1996)
103. New Zealand (19 July 1996)
104. Haiti (31 July 1996)
105. Mongolia (13 August 1996)
106. Palau (30 September 1996)
107. Malaysia (14 October 1996)
108. Brunei Darussalam (5 November 1996)
109. Romania (17 December 1996)
110. Papua New Guinea (14 January 1997)
111. Spain (15 January 1997)
112. Guatemala (11 February 1997)
113. Pakistan (26 February 1997)
114. Russian Federation (12 March 1997)
115. Mozambique (13 March 1997)
116. Solomon Islands (23 June 1997)
117. Equatorial Guinea (21 July 1997)
118. United Kingdom of Great Britain and
     Northern Ireland (25 July 1997)
119. Chile (25 August 1997)
120. Benin (16 October 1997)
121. Portugal (3 November 1997)
122. South Africa (23 December 1997)
123. Gabon (11 March 1998)
124. European Union (1 April 1998)
125. Lao People's Democratic Republic
     (5 June 1998)
126. Suriname (9 July 1998)
127. Nepal (2 November 1998)
128. Belgium (13 November 1998)

129. Poland (13 November 1998)
130. Ukraine (26 July 1999)
131. Vanuatu (10 August 1999)
132. Nicaragua (3 May 2000)
133. Maldives (7 September 2000)
134. Luxembourg (5 October 2000)
135. Serbia (12 March 2001)
136. Bangladesh (27 July 2001)
137. Madagascar (22 August 2001)
138. Hungary (5 February 2002)
139. Armenia (9 December 2002)
140. Qatar (9 December 2002)
141. Tuvalu (9 December 2002)
142. Kiribati (24 February 2003)
143. Albania (23 June 2003)
144. Canada (7 November 2003)
145. Lithuania (12 November 2003)
146. Denmark (16 November 2004)
147. Latvia (23 December 2004)
148. Burkina Faso (25 January 2005)
149. Estonia (26 August 2005)
150. Belarus (30 August 2006)
151. Niue (11 October 2006)
152. Montenegro (23 October 2006)
153. Republic of Moldova (6 February 2007)
154. Lesotho (31 May 2007)
155. Morocco (31 May 2007)
156. Congo (9 July 2008)
157. Liberia (25 September 2008)
158. Switzerland (1 May 2009)
159. Dominican Republic (10 July 2009)
160. Chad (14 August 2009)
161. Malawi (28 September 2010)
162. Thailand (15 May 2011)
163. Ecuador (24 September 2012)
164. Swaziland (24 September 2012)

b.   Agreement relating to the Implementation of Part XI of the Convention

1.   Kenya (29 July 1994)
2.   The former Yugoslav Republic of Macedonia
       (19 August 1994)
3.   Australia (5 October 1994)
4.   Germany (14 October 1994)
5.   Belize (21 October 1994)
6.   Mauritius (4 November 1994)
7.   Singapore (17 November 1994)
8.   Sierra Leone (12 December 1994)
9.   Seychelles (15 December 1994)
10. Lebanon (5 January 1995)
11. Italy (13 January 1995)
12. Cook Islands (15 February 1995)
13. Croatia (5 April 1995)
14. Bolivia (Plurinational State of)
       (28 April 1995)
15. Slovenia (16 June 1995)
16. India (29 June 1995)
17. Paraguay (10 July 1995)
18. Austria (14 July 1995)
19. Greece (21 July 1995)
20. Senegal (25 July 1995)
21. Cyprus (27 July 1995)
22. Bahamas (28 July 1995)
23. Barbados (28 July 1995)
24. Côte d'Ivoire (28 July 1995)
25. Fiji (28 July 1995)
26. Grenada (28 July 1995)
27. Guinea (28 July 1995)
28. Iceland (28 July 1995)
29. Jamaica (28 July 1995)
30. Namibia (28 July 1995)
31. Nigeria (28 July 1995)
32. Sri Lanka (28 July 1995)
33. Togo (28 July 1995)
34. Trinidad and Tobago (28 July 1995)
35. Uganda (28 July 1995)
36. Serbia (28 July 1995)
37. Zambia (28 July 1995)
38. Zimbabwe (28 July 1995)
39. Tonga (2 August 1995)
40. Samoa (14 August 1995)
41. Micronesia (Federated States of)
       (6 September 1995)
42. Jordan (27 November 1995)
43. Argentina (1 December 1995)
44. Nauru (23 January 1996)
45. Republic of Korea (29 January 1996)
46. Monaco (20 March 1996)
47. Georgia (21 March 1996)
48. France (11 April 1996)
49. Saudi Arabia (24 April 1996)
50. Slovakia (8 May 1996)
51. Bulgaria (15 May 1996)

52. Myanmar (21 May 1996)
53. China (7 June 1996)
54. Algeria (11 June 1996)
55. Japan (20 June 1996)
56. Czech Republic (21 June 1996)
57. Finland (21 June 1996)
58. Ireland (21 June 1996)
59. Norway (24 June 1996)
60. Sweden (25 June 1996)
61. Malta (26 June 1996)
62. Netherlands (28 June 1996)
63. Panama (1 July 1996)
64. Mauritania (17 July 1996)
65. New Zealand (19 July 1996)
66. Haiti (31 July 1996)
67. Mongolia (13 August 1996)
68. Palau (30 September 1996)
69. Malaysia (14 October 1996)
70. Brunei Darussalam (5 November 1996)
71. Romania (17 December 1996)
72. Papua New Guinea (14 January 1997)
73. Spain (15 January 1997)
74. Guatemala (11 February 1997)
75. Oman (26 February 1997)
76. Pakistan (26 February 1997)
77. Russian Federation (12 March 1997)
78. Mozambique (13 March 1997)
79. Solomon Islands (23 June 1997)
80. Equatorial Guinea (21 July 1997)
81. Philippines (23 July 1997)
82. United Kingdom of Great Britain
       and Northern Ireland (25 July 1997)
83. Chile (25 August 1997)
84. Benin (16 October 1997)
85. Portugal (3 November 1997)
86. South Africa (23 December 1997)
87. Gabon (11 March 1998)
88. European Union (1 April 1998)
89. Lao People's Democratic Republic
       (5 June 1998)
90. United Republic of Tanzania (25 June 1998)
91. Suriname (9 July 1998)
92. Nepal (2 November 1998)
93. Belgium (13 November 1998)
94. Poland (13 November 1998)
95. Ukraine (26 July 1999)
96. Vanuatu (10 August 1999)
97. Nicaragua (3 May 2000)
98. Indonesia (2 June 2000)
99. Maldives (7 September 2000)
100. Luxembourg (5 October 2000)
101. Bangladesh (27 July 2001)
102. Madagascar (22 August 2001)
103. Costa Rica (20 September 2001)

104. Hungary (5 February 2002)
105. Tunisia (24 May 2002)
106. Cameroon (28 August 2002)
107. Kuwait (2 August 2002)
108. Cuba (17 October 2002)
109. Armenia (9 December 2002)
110. Qatar (9 December 2002)
111. Tuvalu (9 December 2002)
112. Kiribati (24 February 2003)
113. Mexico (10 April 2003)
114. Albania (23 June 2003)
115. Honduras (28 July 2003)
116. Canada (7 November 2003)
117. Lithuania (12 November 2003)
118. Denmark (16 November 2004)
119. Latvia (23 December 2004)
120. Botswana (31 January 2005)
121. Burkina Faso (25 January 2005)
122. Estonia (26 August 2005)
123. Viet Nam (27 April 2006)
124. Belarus (30 August 2006)
125. Niue (11 October 2006)

126. Montenegro (23 October 2006)
127. Republic of Moldova (6 February 2007)
128. Lesotho (31 May 2007)
129. Morocco (31 May 2007)
130. Uruguay (7 August 2007)
131. Brazil (25 October 2007)
132. Cape Verde (23 April 2008)
133. Congo (9 July 2008)
134. Liberia (25 September 2008)
135. Guyana (25 September 2008)
136. Switzerland (1 May 2009)
137. Dominican Republic (10 July 2009)
138. Chad (14 August 2009)
139. Angola (7 September 2010)
140. Malawi (28 September 2010)
141. Thailand (15 May 2011)
142. Ecuador (24 September 2012)
143. Swaziland (24 September 2012)

c. Agreement for the Implementation of the Provisions of the United Nations Convention on the Law of the Sea of 10 December 1982 relating to the Conservation and Management of Straddling Fish Stocks and Highly Migratory Fish Stocks

1. Tonga (31 July 1996)
2. Saint Lucia (9 August 1996)
3. United States of America (21 August 1996)
4. Sri Lanka (24 October 1996)
5. Samoa (25 October 1996)
6. Fiji (12 December 1996)
7. Norway (30 December 1996)
8. Nauru (10 January 1997)
9. Bahamas (16 January 1997)
10. Senegal (30 January 1997)
11. Solomon Islands (13 February 1997)
12. Iceland (14 February 1997)
13. Mauritius (25 March 1997)
14. Micronesia (Federated States of) (23 May 1997)
15. Russian Federation (4 August 1997)
16. Seychelles (20 March 1998)
17. Namibia (8 April 1998)
18. Iran (Islamic Republic of) (17 April 1998)
19. Maldives (30 December 1998)
20. Cook Islands (1 April 1999)
21. Papua New Guinea (4 June 1999)
22. Monaco (9 June 1999)
23. Canada (3 August 1999)
24. Uruguay (10 September 1999)
25. Australia (23 December 1999)
26. Brazil (8 March 2000)
27. Barbados (22 September 2000)
28. New Zealand (18 April 2001)
29. Costa Rica (18 June 2001)
30. Malta (11 November 2001)
31. United Kingdom of Great Britain and Northern Ireland (10 December 2001), (19 December 2003)
32. Cyprus (25 September 2002)
33. Ukraine (27 February 2003)
34. Marshall Islands (19 March 2003)
35. South Africa (14 August 2003)
36. India (19 August 2003)
37. European Union (19 December 2003)
38. Austria (19 December 2003)
39. Belgium (19 December 2003)
40. Denmark (19 December 2003)
41. Finland (19 December 2003)
42. France (19 December 2003)
43. Germany (19 December 2003)
44. Greece (19 December 2003)
45. Ireland (19 December 2003)
46. Italy (19 December 2003)
47. Luxembourg (19 December 2003)
48. Netherlands (19 December 2003)
49. Portugal (19 December 2003)
50. Spain (19 December 2003)
51. Sweden (19 December 2003)
52. Kenya (13 July 2004)
53. Belize (14 July 2005)
54. Kiribati (15 September 2005)
55. Guinea (16 September 2005)
56. Liberia (16 September 2005)
57. Poland (14 March 2006)
58. Slovenia (15 June 2006)
59. Estonia (7 August 2006)
60. Japan (7 August 2006)
61. Trinidad and Tobago (13 September 2006)
62. Niue (11 October 2006)
63. Bulgaria (13 December 2006)
64. Latvia (5 February 2007)
65. Lithuania (1 March 2007)
66. Czech Republic (19 March 2007)
67. Romania (16 July 2007)
68. Republic of Korea (1 February 2008)
69. Palau (26 March 2008)
70. Oman (14 May 2008)
71. Hungary (16 May 2008)
72. Slovakia (6 November 2008)
73. Mozambique (10 December 2008)
74. Panama (16 December 2008)
75. Tuvalu (2 February 2009)
76. Indonesia (28 September 2009)
77. Nigeria (2 November 2009)
78. Saint Vincent and the Grenadines (29 October 2010)
79. Morocco (19 September 2012)
80. Bangladesh (5 November 2012)

3. Declaration by States

a. Ecuador: United Nations Convention on the Law of the Sea - Declaration of 24 September 2012[1]

I.   The Ecuadorian State, pursuant to article 4 of the Constitution of the Republic, which provides that "the territory of Ecuador constitutes a single geographical and historical unit with natural, social and cultural dimensions, the legacy of our forebears and ancestral peoples. This territory includes the continental and maritime space, the adjacent islands, the territorial sea, the Galapagos Archipelago, the soil, the continental shelf, the subsoil and the superjacent continental, island and maritime space. Its boundaries are those established in the treaties in force", confirms the full validity of the Declaration of Santiago on the Maritime Zone, signed in Santiago, Chile, on 18 August 1952, by means of which Chile, Ecuador and Peru declared "... as a norm of their international maritime policy, the exclusive sovereignty and jurisdiction that each of them possesses in respect of the sea adjacent to the coasts of their respective countries, up to a minimum distance of 200 nautical miles from those coasts..." in order ".... to ensure that their peoples have the necessary livelihood conditions and to provide them with the means for their economic development...";

II.   The Ecuadorian State, in accordance with the provisions of the Convention, exercises sovereignty and jurisdiction over the 200 nautical miles that comprise the following maritime spaces:

1. Internal waters, which are the waters on the landward side of the baselines;
2. The territorial sea, which extends from the baselines to a limit not exceeding 12 nautical miles;
3. The exclusive economic zone, which is an area that extends for 188 nautical miles from the outer limits of the territorial sea; and,
4. The continental shelf;

III.   Ecuador shall exercise its sovereign jurisdiction and competence, without limitation or restriction of any type, in the internal waters and the 12 nautical miles of the territorial sea, measured from the baselines. It guarantees the right of coastal and non-coastal countries to continuous and expeditious innocent passage of their ships, with the obligation that they comply with the provisions of the Ecuadorian State, and provided that such passage is not prejudicial to the peace, good order or security of the State;

IV.   In the exclusive economic zone, the Republic of Ecuador shall have the following rights and obligations:

1. Exclusive sovereignty for the purpose of exploring and exploiting, conserving and managing the natural resources, whether living or non-living, of the waters superjacent to the seabed and of the seabed and its subsoil;
2. Exclusive sovereignty for the purposes of the economic exploitation and exploration of the zone, such as the production of energy from the water, marine currents and winds;
3. Exercise of the exclusive right to authorize, regulate and undertake the construction, operation and use of all types of artificial islands, installations and structures within the 200 miles of its maritime territory, including the continental shelf;
4. The other rights and duties laid down in the Convention;
5. All other States, whether coastal or land-locked, enjoy the freedoms of navigation, overflight and the laying of submarine cables and pipelines, subject to the provisions of the Convention.

The other States shall observe and comply with the laws, rules and regulations issued by the Ecuadorian State in its capacity as a coastal State;

---

[1] Attention: Treaty Services of Ministries of Foreign Affairs and of international organizations concerned. Depositary notifications are issued in electronic format only. Depositary notifications are made available to the Permanent Missions to the United Nations in the United Nations Treaty Collection on the Internet at http://treaties.un.org, under "Depositary Notifications (CNs)". In addition, the Permanent Missions, as well as other interested individuals, can subscribe to receive depositary notifications by e-mail through the Treaty Section's "Automated Subscription Services", which is also available at http://treaties.un.org.

V.   With regard to the continental shelf, the Ecuadorian State exercises exclusive sovereign rights for the purposes of exploring, conserving and exploiting its natural resources, and no one may exploit them without its express consent.

The Ecuadorian State declares that, within the timeframe and the conditions set forth in article 76 of the Convention, it will make use of its right to extend its continental shelf to a distance of 350 nautical miles measured from the baselines of the Galapagos Archipelago;

VI.   Ecuador reiterates the full force and validity of Supreme Decree No. 959-A, published on 28 June 1971 in Official Register No. 265 of 13 July 1971, by means of which it established its straight baselines in accordance with international law. It reaffirms that the said lines in the Galapagos Archipelago are determined by the common geological origin of those islands, their historical unity and the fact that they belong to Ecuador, as well as the need to protect and preserve their unique ecosystems. The baselines, from which the maritime spaces described in paragraph II of the present Declaration are measured, are as follows:

1.   Continental baselines:

(a)   The line will start from the point of intersection of the maritime boundary with Colombia with the straight line Punta Manglares (Colombia) - Punta Galera (Ecuador);
(b)   From this point, a straight line passing through Punta Galera and meeting the most northerly point of Isla de la Plata;
(c)   From this point a straight line to Puntilla de Santa Elena;
(d)   A straight line from Puntilla de Santa Elena in the direction of Cabo Blanco (Peru) to the intersection with the geographical parallel that constitutes the maritime boundary with Peru.

2.   Insular baselines:

(a)   From Islote Darwin, a straight line to the north-eastern tip of Isla Pinta;
(b)   A straight line to the most northerly point of Isla Genovesa;
(c)   A straight line passing through Punta Valdizan, Isla San Cristobal, and intersecting the northern extension of the straight line joining the south-eastern tip of Isla Española with Punta Pitt, Isla San Cristobal;
(d)   A straight line from this intersection to the south-eastern tip of Isla Española;
(e)   A straight line to Punta Sur, Isla Santa Maria;
(f)   A straight line passing through the south-eastern tip of Isla Santa Isabela, near Punta Esex, and intersecting the southern extension of the line joining the outermost projecting point of the western coast of Isla Fernandina, approximately in its centre, with the western tip of the southern part of Isla Isabela, in the vicinity of Punta Cristobal;
(g)   From this point of intersection a line passing through the western tip of the southern point of the western coast of Isla Fernandina, approximately in its centre;
(h)   A straight line to Isla Darwin;

VII.   With regard to the delimitation of the maritime spaces adjacent to the continental territory of Ecuador, the State declares that this is determined by the delimitation treaties in force and constituted by the geographical parallels extending from the points where the land boundaries reach the sea;

VIII.   It confirms the full validity of the international instruments applicable to the Galapagos Archipelago, by means of which it has been listed as a United Nations Educational, Scientific and Cultural Organization (UNESCO) Natural Heritage for Humanity site and a biosphere reserve of the UNESCO Man and the Biosphere Programme.

The Ecuadorian State therefore exercises full jurisdiction and sovereignty over the Galapagos Marine Reserve, established by the law on the special regime for the conservation and sustainable development of the province of Galapagos, published in Official Register No. 278 of 18 March 1998, as well as over the Particularly Sensitive Sea area and the "area to be avoided", both established by the International Maritime Organization;

IX.   Ecuador declares that the Gulf of Guayaquil is a historic bay, owing to its traditional use and exploitation by the people of Ecuador, as well as the positive influence of the waters of the Guayas river in generating an ecosystem rich in natural resources;

X.   The Ecuadorian State declares that it has the exclusive right to regulate uses or activities not expressly provided for in the Convention (residual rights and jurisdiction) that relate to its rights within the 200 nautical miles, as well as any future expansion of the said rights;

XI.   It declares that States whose warships, naval auxiliaries, or other vessels or aircraft that, subject to prior notification of and authorization by the Ecuadorian State, may pass through the maritime spaces subject to its sovereignty and jurisdiction, are liable for any damage they cause by polluting the marine environment, pursuant to articles 235 and 236 of the Convention;

XII.   In accordance with the relevant provisions of the Convention, when the same or associated fish stocks are found both within the Ecuadorian 200-mile zone and in a maritime area adjacent to the said zone, the States whose nationals fish for those species in the area adjacent to the Ecuadorian zone must agree with the Ecuadorian State the measures necessary to conserve and protect them, as well as to promote their optimum utilization. In the absence of such agreement, Ecuador reserves to itself the exercise of its rights under article 116 and other provisions of the Convention, as well as all other relevant rules of international law;

XIII.   The Ecuadorian State, in cases where it is party to a commercial contract in the Area of the seabed, will not submit itself to binding commercial arbitration, as this is prohibited by article 422 of its Constitution. In such cases, it will provide prior express notice of the dispute resolution mechanism to which it will submit, provided that this does not involve the transfer of its sovereign jurisdiction.

XIV.   In accordance with article 287 of the Convention, Ecuador chooses, for the settlement of disputes concerning the interpretation or application of the Convention:

1.   The International Tribunal for the Law of the Sea;
2.   The International Court of Justice;
3.   A special tribunal constituted in accordance with Annex VIII, for one or more of the categories of disputes relating to fisheries, protection and preservation of the marine environment, marine scientific research and navigation, including pollution from vessels and by dumping;

XV.   With regard to article 297, paragraphs 2 and 3 of the Convention, the Government of Ecuador will not accept the submission to the procedures provided for in Part XV, section 2, of disputes relating to the exercise of its rights in relation to scientific research, as well as with respect to the regulation of fisheries within the 200 nautical miles, including its discretionary powers for determining the catch, its harvesting capacity, the allocation of surpluses, if any, and the terms and conditions established in its conservation and management laws and regulations;

XVI.   With regard to the provisions of article 297, paragraph 3, subparagraphs (b) (iii) and (c), Ecuador will not accept the validity of any report of the conciliation commission that substitutes its discretion for that of the Ecuadorian State in relation to the use of surplus living resources within its areas of sovereignty and jurisdiction, in application of articles 62, 69 and 70 of the Convention, or whose recommendations entail effects detrimental to Ecuadorian fishing activities;

XVII.   In accordance with article 298 of the Convention, Ecuador declares that it does not accept any of the procedures provided for in Part XV, section 2, with respect to the categories of disputes described in paragraph 1, subparagraphs (a), (b) and (c), of the said article 298;

XVIII. The Ecuadorian State declares, in accordance with articles 5 and 416 of the Constitution of the Republic, that its maritime spaces constitute a *zone of peace*; consequently, no military exercises or manoeuvres of any type, nor any shipping activities that threaten or could threaten peace and security, may be conducted without its express consent.

Furthermore, it hereby declares that prior notification and authorization shall be required for the transit through its maritime spaces of ships powered by nuclear energy or transporting radioactive, toxic, hazardous or harmful substances.

*****

Subsequently, the Government of Ecuador notified the Secretary-General that it wished to clarify that, in respect of paragraph XIII of the aforementioned Declaration, in cases where Ecuador is party to a contract relating to activities in the Area of the seabed, Ecuador recognizes the competence of the Seabed Disputes Chamber of the International Tribunal for the Law of the Sea.

       b.   Argentina: Partial Withdrawal of Declaration with Respect to Article 298[2]

Reference: C.N.622.2012.TREATIES-XXI.6 (Depositary Notification)

UNITED NATIONS CONVENTION ON THE LAW OF THE SEA
MONTEGO BAY, 10 DECEMBER 1982

The Secretary-General of the United Nations, acting in his capacity as depositary, communicates the following:

The above action was effected on 26 October 2012.

(Translation) (Original: Spanish)

[...] in accordance with article 298 of [the] Convention, the Argentine Republic withdraws with immediate effect the optional exceptions to the applicability of section 2 of part XV of the Convention provided for in that article and set forth in its declaration dated 18 October 1995 (deposited on 1 December 1995) to "military activities by government vessels and aircraft engaged in non-commercial service".

7 November 2012

---

[2] Refer to depository notification C.N.425.TREATIES-9/9 of 8 February 1996 (Ratification by Argentina).
Note by the Editor: The notification referred to above was issued in LOS Bulletin 30, pp. 6-8.

II.   LEGAL INFORMATION RELEVANT TO THE UNITED NATIONS
CONVENTION ON THE LAW OF THE SEA

A.   National Legislation

1.   Australia

*Seas and Submerged Lands
(Limits of Continental Shelf) Proclamation 2012*[1]

Seas and Submerged Lands Act 1973

I, QUENTIN BRYCE, Governor-General of the Commonwealth of Australia, acting with the advice of the Federal Executive Council, make the following Proclamation under section 12 of the *Seas and Submerged Lands Act 1973.*

Signed and sealed with the
Great Seal of Australia
On 24 May 2012

Quentin Bryce
Governor-General

By Her Excellency's Command

Nicola Roxon
Attorney-General

---

[1] Federal Register of Legislative Instruments F2012L01081.
Note by the Editor: The list of geographical coordinates of points, specifying the geodetic data were deposited with the Secretary-General under articles 76(9) and 89 of the Convention (see Maritime Zone Notification M.Z.N.92.2012.LOS of 9 November 2012).

Contents

---

[2] Note by the Editor: The entirety of this section can be found at
http://www.un.org/Depts/los/LEGISLATIONANDTREATIES/PDFFILES/DEPOSIT/aus_mzn91_2012_volume_1.pdf.

[3] Note by the Editor: This section can be found at
http://www.un.org/Depts/los/LEGISLATIONANDTREATIES/PDFFILES/DEPOSIT/aus_mzn91_2012_volume_2.pdf.

1   **Name of Proclamation**

This Proclamation is the *Seas and Submerged Lands (Limits of Continental Shelf)* Proclamation 2012.

2   **Commencement**

This Proclamation commences on the day after it is registered.

3   **Repeal**

The Seas and Submerged Lands (Limits of Continental Shelf in the Tasman Sea and South Pacific Ocean) Proclamation 2005 (Federal Register of Legislative Instruments No. F2005L01990) is repealed.

4   **Continental shelf—mainland Australia (including Tasmania, other than Macquarie Island), Lord Howe Island and Norfolk Island**

The outer limit of certain parts of Australia's continental shelf adjacent to the coast of the mainland of Australia (including Tasmania, other than Macquarie Island) and adjacent to the coasts of Lord Howe Island and Norfolk Island is the line specified in Part 1 of Schedule 1.

Note 1   The line is not continuous and is broken in several places as set out in Part 1 of Schedule 1. See the map in Schedule 6 for a general illustration of the line specified in Part 1 of Schedule 1.

Note 2   For information about Part 2 of Schedule 1, see subsection 9 (2).

5   **Continental shelf—Macquarie Island**

The outer limit of Australia's continental shelf adjacent to the coast of Macquarie Island is the line specified in Schedule 2.

Note   See the map in Schedule 6 for a general illustration of the line specified in Schedule 2.

6   **Continental shelf—Heard Island and McDonald Islands**

The outer limit of Australia's continental shelf adjacent to the coasts of Heard Island and McDonald Islands is the line specified in Part 1 of Schedule 3.

Note 1   See the map in Schedule 6 for a general illustration of the line specified in Part 1 of Schedule 3.

Note 2   For information about Part 2 of Schedule 3, see subsection 9 (2).

7   **Continental shelf—Cocos (Keeling) Islands**

The outer limit of Australia's continental shelf adjacent to the coast of Cocos (Keeling) Islands is the line specified in Schedule 4.

Note   See the map in Schedule 6 for a general illustration of the line specified in Schedule 4.

8   **Continental shelf—Christmas Island**

The outer limit of certain parts of Australia's continental shelf adjacent to the coast of Christmas Island is the line specified in Schedule 5.

Note   See the map in Schedule 6 for a general illustration of the line specified in Schedule 5.

9   **Operation of Schedules 1 to 5**

(1)   In Schedules 1 to 5:

     (a)   lines are specified by reference to points; and

     (b)   the columns of an item in a table in which a point is specified set out information about the point; and

     (c)   the information about the point:

         (i)   includes the point identifier shown in the first column of an item in the table (the point identifier is sometimes used in this Proclamation to refer to the point); and

         (ii)   may also include a treaty point reference, which is a reference to how the point is referred to in the relevant treaty for a point mentioned in section 10; and

         (iii)   also includes geographic coordinates for the point (for more about geographic coordinates, see section 11); and

     (d)   the geographic coordinates for a point determine the location of the point for this Proclamation.

Note   For some points mentioned in Schedule 1, the information may include more than one treaty (and more than one treaty point reference).

(2)   In Schedules 1 and 3:

     (a)   the geographic coordinates for a point (and the datum by reference to which they are determined) shown in Part 1 of each Schedule determine the location of the point for this Proclamation; and

     (b)   the geographic coordinates shown in Part 2 of each Schedule:

         (i)   represent the authoritative conversion for some of the points mentioned in Part 1 of each Schedule into the International Terrestrial Reference Frame 2000 (ITRF2000), as defined by the International Earth Rotation and Reference Systems Service at epoch 1 January 2000 in *IERS Technical Note No. 31*; and

         (ii)   are included for the information of readers; and

         (iii)   do not determine the location of those points for this Proclamation; and

         (iv)   are included to clarify the relationship between certain historical datums and ITRF 2000, so that a connection with future datums can be maintained.

10   **Relevant treaties**

The relevant treaty for a point is as follows:

     (a)   for points AUS-CS-1 to AUS-CS-20 in Schedule 1—*Treaty between Australia and the Independent State of Papua New Guinea concerning Sovereignty and Maritime Boundaries in the area between the two Countries, including the area known as Torres Strait, and Related Matters*, Australian Treaty Series 1985 No. 4;

     (b)   for points AUS-CS-101 and AUS-CS-102 in Schedule 1—*Agreement between the Government of* Australia *and the Government of Solomon Islands establishing Certain Sea and Seabed Boundaries*, Australian Treaty Series 1989 No. 12;

     (c)   for points AUS-CS-102 to AUS-CS-123 in Schedule 1 and points HMI-CS-1 to HMI-CS-7 in Schedule 3—*Agreement on Maritime Delimitation between the Government of Australia and the Government of the French Republic*, Australian Treaty Series 1983 No. 3;

     (d)   for points AUS-CS-124 to AUS-CS-150 in Schedule 1 and points MAC-CS-1 to MAC-CS-24 in Schedule 2—*Treaty between the Government of Australia and the Government of New Zealand establishing Certain Exclusive Economic Zone Boundaries and Continental Shelf Boundaries*, Australian Treaty Series 2006 No. 4.

Note 1   For some points mentioned in Schedule 1, more than one treaty is relevant (and more than one treaty point reference is mentioned for the point).

Note 2   No treaty is relevant for Schedule 4 (which relates to Cocos (Keeling) Islands) or Schedule 5 (which relates to Christmas Island).

Note 3   In 2012, the text of a treaty in the Australian Treaty Series was accessible through the Australian Treaties Library on the AustLII website (www.austlii.edu.au).

11   Geographic coordinates

(1)   The following table shows the abbreviation used in this Proclamation for each datum mentioned in the table.

Item	Abbreviation	Datum
1	AGD66	Australian Geodetic Datum 1966
2	ITRF2000	International Terrestrial Reference Frame 2000, as defined by International Earth Rotation and Reference Systems Service at epoch 1 January 2000 in *IERS Technical Note No. 31*
3	WGS72	World Geodetic System 1972
4	WGS84	World Geodetic System 1984

(2)   For this Proclamation, a geographic coordinate is determined by reference to the datum mentioned in Schedules 1 to 5 for the coordinate.

(3)   For this Proclamation, the datums mentioned in subsection (4) are taken to be equivalent.

Note   See *US National Imagery and Mapping Agency, Technical Report—NIMA TR8350.2 Third Edition (including amendments to 23 June 2004)—Department of Defense World Geodetic System 1984—Its Definition and Relationships with Local Geodetic Systems*, in particular Chapters 2.2.1 and 7.

(4)   The datums are:

(a)   WGS84; and

(b)   ITRF2000.

Outer limit of parts of continental shelf adjacent to coasts of mainland Australia (including Tasmania, other than Macquarie Island), Lord Howe Island and Norfolk Island

References to certain points by geographic coordinates in terms of treaty datum or International Terrestrial Reference Frame 2000 (if points not defined by treaty)

Schedule 1

Part 1

Schedule 1   **Outer limit of parts of continental shelf adjacent to coasts of mainland Australia (including Tasmania, other than Macquarie Island), Lord Howe Island and Norfolk Island**
(section 4)

Part 1   References to certain points by geographic coordinates in terms of treaty datum or International Terrestrial Reference Frame 2000 (if points not defined by treaty)

The line:

(a)   commencing at point AUS-CS-1 in the following table and running along the geodesics sequentially connecting each point in the table and ending at the last point mentioned (AUS-CS-123):

Point identifier	Latitude	Longitude	Treaty point reference(s)	Datum
AUS-CS-1	10°50'00.0000"S	139°12'00.0000"E	(a)	AGD66
AUS-CS-2	11°09'00.0000"S	139°23'00.0000"E	(b)	AGD66
AUS-CS-3	10°59'00.0000"S	140°00'00.0000"E	(c)	AGD66
AUS-CS-4	09°46'00.0000"S	142°00'00.0000"E	(d)	AGD66
AUS-CS-5	09°45'24.0000"S	142°03'30.0000"E	(e)	AGD66
AUS-CS-6	09°42'00.0000"S	142°23'00.0000"E	(f)	AGD66
AUS-CS-7	09°40'30.0000"S	142°51'00.0000"E	(g)	AGD66
AUS-CS-8	09°40'00.0000"S	143°00'00.0000"E	(h)	AGD66
AUS-CS-9	09°33'00.0000"S	143°05'00.0000"E	(i)	AGD66
AUS-CS-10	09°33'00.0000"S	143°20'00.0000"E	(j)	AGD66
AUS-CS-11	09°24'00.0000"S	143°30'00.0000"E	(k)	AGD66
AUS-CS-12	09°22'00.0000"S	143°48'00.0000"E	(l)	AGD66
AUS-CS-13	09°30'00.0000"S	144°15'00.0000"E	(m)	AGD66
AUS-CS-14	09°51'00.0000"S	144°44'00.0000"E	(n)	AGD66
AUS-CS-15	12°20'00.0000"S	146°30'00.0000"E	(o)	AGD66
AUS-CS-16	12°38'30.0000"S	147°08'30.0000"E	(p)	AGD66
AUS-CS-17	13°10'30.0000"S	148°05'00.0000"E	(q)	AGD66

Schedule 6 **Map**
(sections 4 to 8)

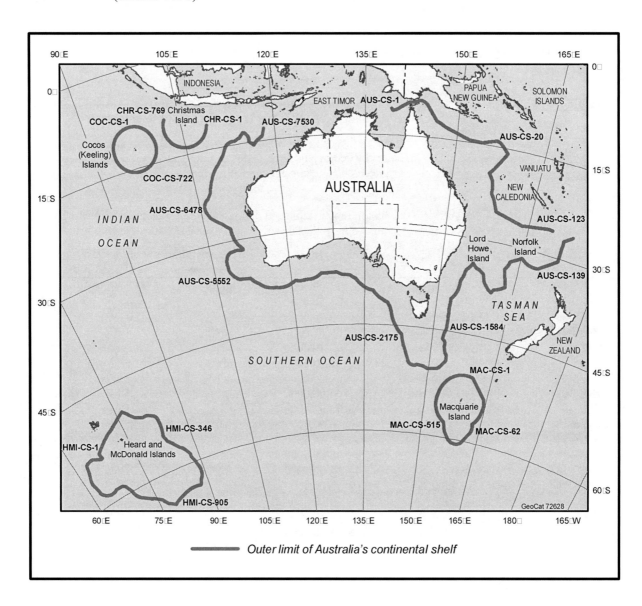

Outer limit of Australia's continental shelf

Note

1. All legislative instruments and compilations are registered on the Federal Register of Legislative Instruments kept under the *Legislative Instruments Act 2003*. See www.comlaw.gov.au.

EXPLANATORY STATEMENT

Seas and Submerged Lands (Limits of Continental Shelf) Proclamation 2012

Issued by the Authority of the Attorney-General

This explanatory statement relates to the *Seas and Submerged Lands (Limits of Continental Shelf) Proclamation 2012* made by the Governor-General on 24 May 2012 under section 12 of the *Seas and Submerged Lands Act 1973* (the Act).

The Proclamation is a legislative instrument for the purposes of the *Legislative Instruments Act 2003*.

Authority

Section 12 of the Act provides that the Governor-General may, from time to time, by Proclamation declare, not inconsistently with Article 76 of the *United Nations Convention on the Law of the Sea* (UNCLOS) or any relevant international agreement to which Australia is a party, the limits of the whole or any part of the continental shelf of Australia.

Purpose

The purpose of the Proclamation is to confirm the outer limits of a considerable area of the Australian continental shelf. This includes those areas of continental shelf beyond 200 nautical miles from the territorial sea baseline (the extended continental shelf) based upon the recommendations of the United Nations Commission on the Limits of the Continental Shelf (the Commission) established under Annex II to UNCLOS. As a matter of both international law and Australian law, the continental shelf inures to Australia irrespective of the Proclamation of its outer limits. However, the Proclamation will serve to provide certainty as to the location of those limits.

Legislation affected by the Proclamation

The Proclamation repeals the *Seas and Submerged Lands (Limits of Continental Shelf in the Tasman Sea and South Pacific Ocean) Proclamation 2005*. The boundary declared by the repealed Proclamation is incorporated in the Proclamation.

Background

Article 76 of UNCLOS provides that the continental shelf of a coastal State comprises the sea-bed and subsoil of the submarine areas that extend beyond its territorial sea throughout the natural prolongation of its land territory either to the outer edge of the continental margin or to a distance of 200 nautical miles from the territorial sea baseline, whichever is the greater.

Article 76 further provides that in the former case, the extended continental shelf claimed by a coastal State may not exceed the most distant of a line which is 350 nautical miles from the territorial sea baseline or a line which is 100 nautical miles from the 2,500 metre isobath. The 2,500 metre isobath is a line connecting sea depths of 2,500 metres.

On November 2004, in accordance with paragraph 8 of article 76 of UNCLOS, Australia submitted scientific data and information on its extended continental shelf to the Commission. On 9 April 2008, the Commission adopted recommendations in response to Australia's submission. On the basis of those recommendations, Australia is now able to declare the outer limit of most of its continental shelf. Therefore, in addition to those areas of continental shelf within 200 nautical miles, the Proclamation will confirm Australia's jurisdiction over an extended continental shelf of approximately 2.56 million square kilometres in nine discrete areas:

(i)	Lord Howe Rise, east of Lord Howe Island and west of Norfolk Island;
(ii)	Three Kings Ridge, east of Norfolk Island;
(iii)	South Tasman Rise, south of Tasmania;
(iv)	Macquarie Ridge, south of Macquarie Island;
(v)	Great Australian Bight off South Australia;
(vi)	Kerguelen Plateau, south east of Heard Island and the McDonald Islands;

(vii)   Naturaliste Plateau, off the south west coast of Western Australia and west of Cape Leeuwin;

(viii)   Wallaby Exmouth Plateaus off the mid west coast of Western Australia; and

(ix)   the Argo area off the northwest coast of Western Australia.

Contents of the Proclamation

The limits of the continental shelf are defined using geographic coordinates set out in Schedules appended to the Proclamation. Further detail on the content of the Proclamation and its six Schedules is set out in the Attachment.

Authority: Section 12 of the *Seas and Submerged Lands Act 1973*

Details of the *Seas and Submerged Lands (Limits of Continental Shelf) Proclamation 2012*

Sections 1 and 2 provide for the name and commencement date of the Proclamation.

Section 3 repeals the *Seas and Submerged Lands (Limits of Continental Shelf in the Tasman Sea and South Pacific Ocean) Proclamation 2005*. The boundary that is the subject of the repealed proclamation is incorporated into the Proclamation.

Sections 4 to 8 define the outer limit of Australia's continental shelf, as follows:

(i)	section 4 provides that the continental shelf limit around mainland Australia (including Tasmania, other than Macquarie Island), Lord Howe Island and Norfolk Island is the line defined in Part 1 of Schedule 1;
(ii)	section 5 provides that the continental shelf limit adjacent to Macquarie Island is the line defined in Schedule 2;
(iii)	section 6 provides that the continental shelf limit adjacent to Heard Island and the McDonald Islands is the line defined in Part 1 of Schedule 3;
(iv)	section 7 provides that the continental shelf limit adjacent to Cocos (Keeling) Islands is the line defined in Schedule 4; and
(v)	section 8 provides that the continental shelf limit adjacent to Christmas Island is the line defined in Schedule 5.

Section 9 describes the operation of Schedules 1 to 5. Subsection 9(1) explains that the lines in Schedules 1 to 5 are defined by a series of points. Each point is described by a unique identifier, such that the points are numbered consecutively as follows:

(i)	AUS-CS-1 to AUS-CS-7530 in Schedule 1;
(ii)	MAC-CS-1 to MAC-CS-1095 in Schedule 2;
(iii)	HMI-CS-1 to HMI-CS-1736 in Schedule 3;
(iv)	COC-CS-1 to COC-CS-1444 in Schedule 4; and
(v)	CHR-CS-1 to CHR-CS-769 in Schedule 5.

Subsection 9(1) also notes that the Schedules provide the geographic coordinates (latitude and longitude) of each point, the geodetic datum by which these coordinates were derived and treaty point references, where relevant. A treaty point is the primary reference for the definition of the limit of the continental shelf agreed in a treaty between Australia and another country. The treaty point reference is the identifier given to the point in the relevant treaty. Where more than one treaty is relevant, treaty point references are provided for each relevant treaty.

Section 10 lists the treaties between Australia and another country that are relevant in establishing the outer limit. The list comprises one treaty with each of Papua New Guinea, the Solomon Islands, France and New Zealand.

Geodetic datums are coordinate reference systems that permit the precise location on the Earth's surface of the geographic co-ordinates set out in the Schedules.

Section 11 sets out the four different datums which are utilised in the Proclamation to derive the geographic coordinates of points, namely the Australian Geodetic Datum 1966 (AGD66), the International Terrestrial Reference Frame 2000 (ITRF 2000) and the World Geodetic Systems 1972 and 1984 (WGS72 and WGS84 respectively). The datum most commonly used throughout the Proclamation is the ITRF2000. However, where a particular point in the Schedules is sourced in a bilateral treaty which utilises a different datum, the latter datum is used as the coordinates specified in the treaty are determinative of the location of the point.

Schedules 1 and 3 have two Parts. Part 1 of each Schedule includes certain points which are derived by reference to the AGD66 or WGS72. Part 2 of each Schedule provides additional geographic coordinates based on the ITRF 2000 for the same points. These additional coordinates represent the authoritative conversion into the ITRF 2000 and are provided for information only.

Additional coordinates based on the ITRF2000 are not provided for points determined by reference to the WGS84. Section 11 provides that for the purposes of the Proclamation, the ITRF2000 is taken to be equivalent to the WGS84.

Schedule 6 is a map depicting the limits defined in Schedules 1 to 5.

<u>Areas not included in the Proclamation</u>

Three areas of Australian continental shelf are not covered by the Proclamation. In the first two of these areas, not all of the boundary between Australia's continental shelf and that of the opposite States has been formally agreed.

First, the Proclamation does not cover the outer limit of the continental shelf to the north of Australia between (in the west) the northern most point of the extended continental shelf in the Argo area and (in the east) the westerly end of the seabed boundary agreed with Papua New Guinea (Treaty with the Independent State of Papua New Guinea concerning Sovereignty and Maritime Boundaries in the Area between the Two Countries, Including the area known as Torres Strait and Related Matters, [1985] Australian Treaty Series (ATS) 4).

The Government decided not to proclaim the outer limit in this area until the totality of the boundary between those two points has been agreed. The area in question is the subject of a number of treaties between Australia and Indonesia and Australia and East Timor. The western part of this area is covered by the seabed element of the 1997 Maritime Delimitation Treaty with Indonesia (Treaty between the Government of Australia and the Government of the Republic of Indonesia establishing an Exclusive Economic Zone Boundary and Certain Seabed Boundaries [1997] Australian Treaties Not In Force 4). While that Treaty has been signed, it has not yet been brought into force.

The middle part of the area is the subject of a number of treaties with East Timor and, in particular, the Timor Sea Treaty (Timor Sea Treaty between the Government of East Timor and the Government of Australia, [2003] ATS 13 and the Treaty Between Australia and the Democratic Republic of Timor-Leste on Certain Maritime Arrangements in the Timor Sea, [2007] ATS 12. These treaties put in place provisional arrangements concerning the continental shelf, including the Joint Petroleum Development Area, and a moratorium on the assertion of maritime claims between the Parties.

The unproclaimed area also includes the 1971 and 1972 seabed treaties with Indonesia (Agreement between the Government of the Commonwealth of Australia and the Government of the Republic of Indonesia establishing Certain Seabed Boundaries [1973] ATS 31 and the Agreement between the Government of the Commonwealth of Australia and the Government of the Republic of Indonesia establishing Certain Seabed Boundaries in the Area of the Timor and Arafura Seas, supplementary to the Agreement of 18 May 1971 [1973] ATS 32).

Secondly, the Proclamation does not define the outer limit of the continental shelf in the Three Kings Ridge area in the New Caledonia region. This is because there is potential overlap between the extended continental shelf of Australia and that of France in this region. The limit of the continental shelf in this area may be the subject of discussions between France and Australia, and possibly New Zealand, at a later date.

The third area is that adjacent to the Australian Antarctic Territory (AAT). Due to the special political and legal status of Antarctica, and in light of the Commission's acceptance of Australia's request to the Commission not to consider for the time being the data submitted on the continental shelf adjacent to the AAT, the Proclamation does not define the limits of Australia's continental shelf adjacent to the AAT.

The absence of a proclamation for these areas does not affect the legal status of the continental shelf. As a matter of both international law and Australian law, the continental shelf inures to Australia irrespective of the Proclamation of its outer limits. However, the Proclamation will serve to provide certainty as to the location of those limits.

Additionally, two small areas of continental shelf examined by the Commission remain outstanding. One of these areas is located in the north western part of the Wallaby Exmouth Plateaus submission area and the other in the eastern part of the Kerguelen Plateau submission area. Their total area is approximately 80,000 square kilometres. Securing these areas will require a new or revised submission to the Commission that addresses specific matters raised by the Commission in its recommendations.

Statement of Compatibility with Human Rights

Prepared in accordance with Part 3 of the Human Rights (Parliamentary Scrutiny) Act 2011

Seas and Submerged Lands (Limits of Continental Shelf) Proclamation 2012

The *Seas and Submerged Lands (Limits of Continental Shelf) Proclamation 2012* is compatible with the human rights and freedoms recognised or declared in the international instruments listed in section 3 of the *Human Rights (Parliamentary Scrutiny) Act 2011*.

Overview of the Bill/Legislative Instrument

Section 12 of the *Seas and Submerged Lands Act 1973* provides that the Governor-General may, from time to time, by Proclamation declare, not inconsistently with Article 76 of the United Nations Convention on the Law of the Sea or any relevant international agreement to which Australia is a party, the limits of the whole or any part of the continental shelf. The *Seas and Submerged Lands (Limits of Continental Shelf) Proclamation 2012* confirms the outer limit of a considerable area of the Australian continental shelf.

Human rights implications

The *Seas and Submerged Lands (Limits of Continental Shelf) Proclamation 2012* does not engage any of the applicable rights or freedoms.

Conclusion

The *Seas and Submerged Lands (Limits of Continental Shelf) Proclamation 2012* is compatible with human rights as it does not raise any human rights issues.

2.   China

*"Statement of the Government of the People's Republic of China On the
Baselines of the Territorial Sea of Diaoyu Dao and Its Affiliated Islands",
10 September 2012[4]*

In accordance with the *Law of the People's Republic of China on the Territorial Sea and the Contiguous Zone* adopted and promulgated on 25 February 1992, the Government of the People's Republic of China hereby announces the baselines of the territorial sea adjacent to Diaoyu Dao and its affiliated islands of the People's Republic of China.

I. The baselines of the sea adjacent to Diaoyu Dao, Huangwei Yu, Nanxiao Dao, Beixiao Dao, Bei Yu and Fei Yu are composed of all the straight lines joining the points listed below:

1.	Diaoyu Dao 1	25°44. 1′N	123°27. 5′E
2.	Diaoyu Dao 2	25°44. 2′N	123°27. 4′E
3.	Diaoyu Dao 3	25°44. 4′N	123°27. 4′E
4.	Diaoyu Dao 4	25°44. 7′N	123°27. 5′E
5.	Haitun Dao	25°55. 8′N	123°40. 7′E
6.	Xiahuya Dao	25°55. 8′N	123°41. 1′E
7.	Haixing Dao	25°55. 6′N	123°41. 3′E
8.	Huangwei Yu	25°55. 4′N	123°41. 4′E
9.	Haigui Dao	25°55. 3′N	123°41. 4′E
10.	Changlong Dao	25°43. 2′N	123°33. 4′E
11.	Nanxiao Dao	25°43. 2′N	123°33. 2′E
12.	Changyu Dao	25°44. 0′N	123°27. 6′E
1.	Diaoyu Dao 1	25°44. 1′N	123°27. 5′E

---

[4] Original: Chinese. Translation provided by the Permanent Mission of the People's Republic of China to the United Nations. Transmitted by note verbale dated 13 September 2012 from the Permanent Mission of the People's Republic of China to the United Nations addressed to the Secretariat of the United Nations.
Deposited with the Secretary-General under article 16(2) of the Convention (see Maritime Zone Notification M.Z.N.89.2012.LOS of 21 September 2012).

II. The baselines of the territorial sea adjacent to Chiwei Yu are composed of all the straight lines joining the adjacent base points listed below:

1.	Chiwei Yu	25°55. 3′N	124°33. 7′E
2.	Wangchi Dao	25°55. 2′N	124°33. 2′E
3.	Xiaochiwei Dao	25°55. 3′N	124°33. 3′E
4.	Chibeibei Dao	25°55. 5′N	124°33. 5′E
5.	Chibeidong Dao	25°55. 5′N	124°33. 7′E
1.	Chiwei Yu	25°55. 3′N	124°33. 7′E

III. COMMUNICATIONS BY STATES

1. United Republic of Tanzania

Charts and Coordinates showing Straight Baselines of the United Republic of Tanzania[5]

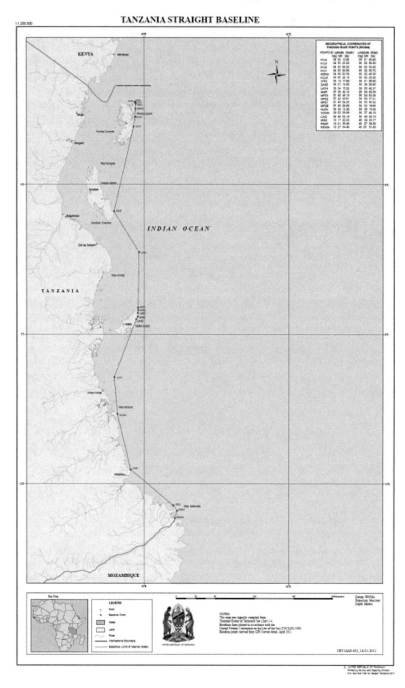

TANZANIA STRAIGHT BASELINE

[5] Transmitted by note verbale dated 2 August 2012 from the Permanent Mission of the United Republic of Tanzania to the United Nations addressed to the Secretary-General of the United Nations.
Deposited with the Secretary-General under article 16(2) of the Convention (see Maritime Zone Notification M.Z.N.93.2013.LOS of 7 January 2013).

GEOGRAPHICAL COORDINATES OF TANZANIA BASE POINTS (WGS84)					
POINTS ID	Latitude (South)			Longitude (East)		
	Deg	Min	Sec	Deg	Min	Sec
KIU4	4	53	12.9	39	51	56.8
KIU3	4	53	23.2	39	52	8.5
KIU2	4	53	59.2	39	52	33.4
KIU1	4	55	5.9	39	52	55.7
MZNG	4	59	3.3	39	52	45.3
KOJA	5	5	26.18	39	52	25.26
VITO	5	13	17.6	39	51	8.9
ZANZ	6	21	18.9	39	35	0.8
LATH	6	54	15.26	39	55	42.37
MAFI	7	38	42.16	39	54	52.55
MFE3	7	40	46.1	39	54	53.24
MFE2	7	42	48.61	39	54	37.41
MFE1	7	45	59.35	39	53	56.52
MFSE	7	48	8.99	39	53	19.64
NJOV	8	34	12.42	39	35	15.44
SONM	9	3	59.96	39	37	46.18
LIND	9	48	50.19	39	48	50.19
MSI2	10	17	22.23	40	24	33.17
RMAT	10	21	38.4	40	27	38.3
RMWA	10	27	54.4	40	25	53.3

2. Argentina

*Letter dated 8 August 2012 from the Permanent Mission of Argentina to the United Nations,
Ministry for Foreign Affairs and Worship addressed to the Secretary-General of the United Nations
in reference to the communication by the United Kingdom of Great Britain and Northern Ireland[6]*

Sir,

Further to the statement made by Argentina to the Commission on the Limits of the Continental Shelf on 26 August 2009 (see document CLCS/64, paragraph 74), I have the honour to write to you in reference to note verbale No. 84/09 of 6 August 2009 from the United Kingdom of Great Britain and Northern Ireland.

The Argentine Republic rejects in its entirety the content of the aforementioned note verbale from the United Kingdom of Great Britain and Northern Ireland.

At the same time, the Argentine Republic reiterates the content of its note of 20 August 2009, in which it objected to the British submission to the Commission concerning the Malvinas Islands, South Georgia Islands and South Sandwich Islands, and recalls that those archipelagos and the surrounding maritime areas are an integral part of the national territory of the Argentine Republic and that, being illegally occupied by the United Kingdom, they are the subject of a sovereignty dispute between the two countries, which has been repeatedly recognized in declarations by the United Nations and other international forums and organizations.

The Argentine Republic reaffirms its rights to sovereignty over the Malvinas Islands, South Georgia Islands and South Sandwich Islands and the surrounding maritime areas and over the Argentine Antarctic Sector. Furthermore, it rejects all claims of sovereignty by the United Kingdom of Great Britain and Northern Ireland over Antarctic Territory.

The Argentine Republic requests that this note be circulated among the States members of the Commission on the Limits of the Continental Shelf, the States parties to the United Nations Convention on the Law of the Sea and the other States Members of the United Nations. It further requests that this note be posted on the website of the Division for Ocean Affairs and the Law of the Sea of the Office of Legal Affairs of the United Nations.

[…]

(*Signed*) Mateo Estremé

Minister

Chargé d'affaires a.i.

[6] Original: Spanish.

3. South Africa, France and Madagascar

Trilateral Declaration on the Limits of the Continental Shelf, 26 June 2012[7]

CONSIDERING that the Republic of South Africa, the French Republic and the Republic of Madagascar are parties to the 1982 United Nations Convention on the Law of the Sea (hereinafter the 'Convention'),

CONSCIOUS that the Republic of South Africa, the French Republic and the Republic of Madagascar are desirous to extend their respective continental shelves,

RECALLING that the Republic of Madagascar made a submission to the Commission on the Limits of the Continental Shelf pursuant to Article 76 of the Convention in April 2011 (hereinafter the 'Madagascar Submission'),

RECALLING ALSO that the Republic of South Africa and the French Republic made a joint partial submission to the Commission on the Limits of the Continental Shelf pursuant to Article 76 of the Convention in May 2009 (hereinafter the 'South Africa/French joint submission'),

NOTING that the Republic of South Africa and the French Republic wish to supplement the joint submission,

RECALLING the provisions of Article 76(10) of the Convention, Rule 46(2) of the Rules of Procedure and Annex I of the Rules of Procedure,

the participants hereby declare as follows:

1. The participants understand that the submissions of their respective Governments to the Commission on the Limits of the Continental Shelf (hereinafter the 'Commission') and the consideration of the respective submissions by the Commission are without prejudice to any future delimitation.

2. The participants agree that the Commission may consider any overlapping claims in the respective submissions on the understanding that the submissions and the recommendations of the Commission on any such overlapping claim will not prejudice any future boundary delimitation process between the respective Governments.

Done in New York, on this ..... day of ....

....

H.E. Baso Sangqu
Ambassador Extraordinary and Plenipotentiary Permanent Representative
The Republic of South Africa

....

H.E. Gerard Araud
Ambassador Extraordinary and Plenipotentiary Permanent Representative
The French Republic

....

H.E. Zina Andrianarivelo-Razafy
Ambassador Extraordinary and Plenipotentiary Permanent Representative
The Republic of Madagascar

---

[7] Original: French.
Transmitted by note verbale dated 8 August 2012 from the Permanent Mission of Madagascar to the United Nations addressed to the Secretariat of the United Nations which indicates that this declaration was signed on 26 June 2012.

4.   Iran (Islamic Republic of)

*Note verbale dated 14 August 2012 addressed to the Secretary-General of the United Nations
concerning the deposit by the Kingdom of Saudi Arabia of the list of geographical
coordinates of points in the Red Sea, Gulf of Aqaba and the Persian Gulf*

No. 692

The Permanent Mission of the Islamic Republic of Iran to the United Nations […] with reference to the communication No. M.Z.N.77.2010.LOS dated 25 March 2010 regarding the deposit by the Kingdom of Saudi Arabia on 5 March 2010 of lists of geographical coordinates of points defining the baselines of the Kingdom of Saudi Arabia in the Red Sea, Gulf of Aqaba and the Persian Gulf, and pursuant to the Note No. 1596 dated 22 December 2010 from the Permanent Mission of the Islamic Republic of Iran to the United Nations, has the honor to inform that the Islamic Republic of Iran carefully studied the above-mentioned document and its annexes, and based on that examination, would like to state the following:

The Government of the Islamic Republic of Iran reserves its position as to the validity under customary international law of the Saudi baselines set out in the mentioned document; under relevant customary international law as codified in the 1958 Convention on the Territorial Sea and the Contiguous Zone, and reaffirmed in the 1982 United Nations Convention on the Law of the Sea: "In localities where the coastline is deeply indented and cut into, or if there is a fringe of islands along the coast in its immediate vicinity, the method of straight baselines joining appropriate points may be employed in drawing the baseline from which the breadth of territorial sea is measured". However, "The drawing of such baselines must not depart to any appreciable extent from the general direction of the coast, and the sea areas lying within the lines must be sufficiently closely linked to the land domain to be subject to the regime of internal waters".

The Islamic Republic of Iran notes that a number of basepoints, particularly basepoints 3, 5, 6 and 8, identified by Saudi Arabia in defining the Saudi baselines in the Persian Gulf are located in the open waters, and therefore, contravene the relevant rules of international law of the sea as mentioned above.

Hence the Islamic Republic of Iran underlines that the method used by Saudi Arabia to define its baselines in the Persian Gulf is not in conformity with international law of the sea and stresses that any consequences arising from it would not be acceptable.

The Permanent Mission of the Islamic Republic of Iran requests the Secretary General of the United Nations to have this note issued as a document of the United Nations in accordance with the established procedures of DOALOS.

[…]

5.   United Kingdom of Great Britain and Northern Ireland

*Note verbale dated 23 August 2012 from the Permanent Mission of the United Kingdom
to the United Nations addressed to the Secretary-General of the United Nations
in reference to the communication by the Republic of Argentina*

Note No: 273/12

The Permanent Mission of the United Kingdom of Great Britain and Northern Ireland […] has the honour to refer to the note of 8 August 2012 from the Permanent Mission of the Republic of Argentina to the United Nations (336/2012).

The United Kingdom reaffirms the views conveyed in its Note of 6 August 2009 (84/09), a copy of which is attached for ease of reference. The United Kingdom has no doubt about its sovereignty over the Falkland Island and over South Georgia and the South Sandwich Islands and their respective surrounding maritime areas. Nor, recalling Article IV of the Antarctic Treaty, does the United Kingdom recognise Argentina's claim to territory in Antarctica and consequently does not recognise that Argentina has any rights over the seabed and subsoil of the submarine areas appurtenant to Antarctica (as defined in the Antarctic Treaty, 1959).

Consequently, the United Kingdom expects that the Commission on the Limits of the Continental Shelf will not consider those parts of Argentina's submission that relate to areas appurtenant to the Falkland Islands, South Georgia and South Sandwich Islands (as detailed it its note of 6 August 2009), or which relate to areas appurtenant to Antarctica.

The Government of the United Kingdom requests that this Note be circulated to the Members of the Commission on the Limits of the Continental Shelf, States Parties to the United Nations Convention on the Law of the Sea, and other Members States of the United Nations, and also requests that the Note be posted on the website of the Division for Ocean Affairs and the Law of the Sea of the Office of Legal Affairs of the United Nations.

   […]

....

Note No: 84/09

The Permanent Mission of the United Kingdom of Great Britain and Northern Ireland […] with reference to his communication of 1 May 2009, CLCS.25.2009.LOS (Continental Shelf Notification), regarding receipt of the submission made by the Argentine Republic to the Commission on the Limits of the Continental Shelf, and to the contents of this submission, has the honour to convey the following:

The Falkland Islands and South Georgia and the South Sandwich Islands

The United Kingdom has no doubt about its sovereignty over the Falkland Islands, and over South Georgia and the South Sandwich Islands and the surrounding maritime areas.

The principle of self-determination, enshrined in the UN Charter, underlies the United Kingdom's position on the sovereignty of the Falkland Islands. There can be no negotiations on the sovereignty of the Falkland Islands unless and until such time as the Falkland Islanders so wish. The Islanders regularly make it clear that they have no wish either to lose British sovereignty or to become independent.

The United Kingdom would like to point out that it exercises control over the continental shelf up to 200 nautical miles from the coast of each of these Overseas Territories, in accordance with the United Kingdom's Declaration on Maritime Jurisdiction around the Falkland Islands of 29 October 1986, and its Proclamation of Maritime Zone around South Georgia and the South Sandwich Islands of 1993. The United Kingdom therefore rejects those parts of Argentina's submission which claim rights to the seabed and subsoil of the submarine areas appurtenant to the Falkland Islands, South Georgia and the South Sandwich Islands, and requests that the Commission does not examine those parts of the Argentine submission - i.e. any fixed points greater than RA-481, except between fixed points RA-3458 and RA-3840.

Antarctica

The United Kingdom recalls the principles and objectives shared by the Antarctic Treaty and UNCLOS, and the importance of the Antarctic system and UNCLOS working in harmony and thereby ensuring the continuing peaceful cooperation, security and stability in the Antarctic area.

Recalling Article IV of the Antarctic Treaty, the United Kingdom does not recognise Argentina's claim to territory in Antarctica and consequently does not recognise that Argentina has any rights over the seabed and subsoil of the submarine areas appurtenant to Antarctica (as defined in the Antarctic Treaty, 1959).

The United Kingdom noted in its Note 168/08 of 9 May 2008 that, as regards Antarctica, it was open to the States concerned to submit information pertaining to Antarctica to the Commission, which would not be examined by it for the time being, or to make a partial submission not including such areas of continental shelf, for which a submission may be made later, notwithstanding the provisions regarding the ten-year period established by article 4 of Annex II to UNCLOS and the subsequent decision on its application taken by the Eleventh Meeting of States Parties to UNCLOS. The United Kingdom took the latter course.

Taking account of the paragraphs above, and consistent with the approach taken by the United Kingdom and other Parties to the Antarctic Treaty, the United Kingdom expects that the Commission will not, for the time being, take any action on that portion of the Argentine submission relating to areas of the seabed and subsoil appurtenant to Antarctica, i.e., all fixed points greater than RA-3840.

The United Kingdom has no objection to the examination by the Commission of the remainder of the Argentine submission, i.e. up to, and including, fixed point RA-481 and between fixed points RA-3458 and RA-3840.

The Government of the United Kingdom requests that this Note be circulated to the Members of the Commission on the Limits of the Continental Shelf, States Parties to the United Nations Convention on the Law of the Sea, and other Member States of the United Nations, and also requests that the Note be posted on the website of the Division for Ocean Affairs and the Law of the Sea of the Office of Legal Affairs of the United Nations.

[…]

6 August 2009

6.   <u>Japan</u>

Note verbale dated 24 September 2012 from the Permanent Mission of Japan to the United Nations addressed to the Secretary-General of the United Nations in respect of a chart and the list of geographical coordinates deposited by the People's Republic of China

PM/12/303

The Permanent Mission of Japan to the United Nations […] with reference to communication No. M.Z.N.89.2012.LOS dated 21 September 2012 has the honour to inform the latter of the position of the Government of Japan concerning the deposit of a chart and a list of geographical coordinates of point made by the People's Republic of China with regard to the baselines for the territorial sea of the Senkaku Islands.

The People's Republic of China deposited the chart and the list of geographical coordinates on 13 September 2012. Such unilateral action has no ground under international law including within the United Nations Convention on the Law of the Sea. This action by the People's Republic of China concerning the Senkaku Islands, a part of the territory of Japan, is totally unacceptable and legally invalid.

There is no doubt that the Senkaku Islands are an inherent part of the territory of Japan in light of historical facts and based upon international law. The Senkaku Islands are under the valid control of the Government of Japan. There exists no issue of territorial sovereignty to be resolved concerning the Senkaku Islands.

The Permanent Mission of Japan has further the honor to request the Secretary-General that this note verbale be transmitted to all Member States of the United Nations and all States Parties to the United Nations Convention on the Law of the Sea.

[…]

7. Ecuador

Nautical Chart IOA42 "Maritime Boundary Ecuador-Colombia"[8]

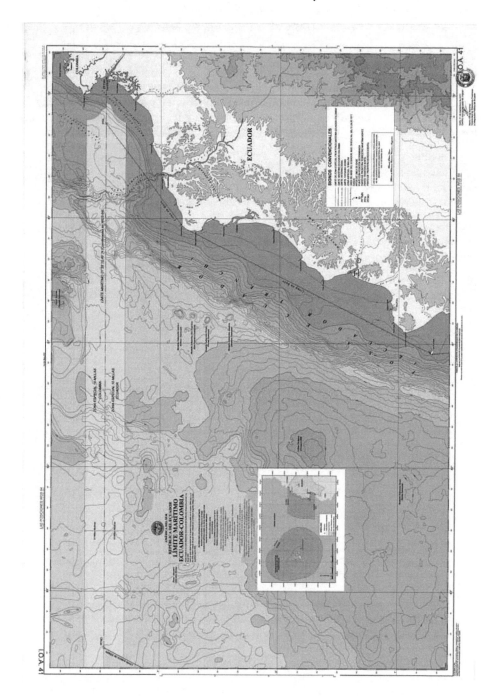

[8] Original: Spanish. Translation provided by the Permanent Mission of Ecuador to the United Nations.
Transmitted by note verbale dated 22 September 2012 from the Permanent Mission of Ecuador to the United Nations addressed to the Secretary-General of the United Nations.
Deposited with the Secretary-General under articles 16(2) and 75(2) of the Convention (see Maritime Zone Notification M.Z.N.90.2012.LOS of 10 October 2012).

8. Saudi Arabia

Note verbale dated 7 October 2012 from the Permanent Mission of the Kingdom of Saudi Arabia to the United Nations addressed to the Secretary-General of the United Nations[2]

The Permanent Mission of the Kingdom of Saudi Arabia to the United Nations […] brings to H.E.'s attention that on Wednesday, 6/9/1443 AH 25/07/2012 AD at 08:53 an Iranian helicopter has spun several times above the rig drill site (ADC-38) in the region of Al-Hasba field, and the rig drill site number (NRL-337) in the same area.

In addition, on Thursday, 7/9/1433 AH 26/07/2012 AD at 07:15, two Iranian military boats intercepted and stopped a boat of one of the Saudi ARAMCO's contractors in ARABIA field area. These two fields are located in the Saudi submerged region pursuant to the the border line that separates the submerged areas between Saudi Arabia and the Islamic Republic of Iran in accordance with the agreement concluded between the two countries on 02/08/1388 AH, corresponding to 10/24/1968 AD.

The Government of Saudi Arabia has protested against these transgressions and demanded the Government of the Islamic Republic of Iran to ensure non-recurrence of these transgressions (Memorandum of the Saudi Foreign Ministry No. 7/2/1/327421 dated 11/20/1433 AH 10/06/2012 AD addressed to the Ministry of Foreign Affairs of the Republic Islamic Iran (copy of which is attached); and that the Government of the Kingdom of Saudi Arabia reserves all rights to take whatever action it deems appropriate to protect its waters and its oil facilities. Furthermore, the Kingdom of Saudi Arabia holds the Iranian authorities fully responsible for all consequences.

The Permanent Mission of the Kingdom of Saudi Arabia requests that His Excellency the Secretary-General of the United Nations distributes this note and the attached protest note of the Saudi Ministry of Foreign Affairs to all Member States; and to publish it in the next edition of the DOALOS.

[…]

....

The Ministry of Foreign Affairs of the Kingdom of Saudi Arabia presents its compliments to the Ministry of Foreign Affairs of the friendly Islamic Republic of Iran;

The Saudi Ministry of Foreign Affairs would like to bring to the attention of the Ministry of Foreign Affairs of the Islamic Republic of Iran that on Wednesday, 6/9/1443 AH 25/07/2012 AD at 08:53 an Iranian helicopter has spun several times above the rig drill site (ADC-38) in the region of Al-Hasba field, and the rig drill site number (NRL-337) in the same area.

In addition, on Thursday, 7/9/1433 AH 26/07/2012 AD at 07:15, two Iranian military boats intercepted and stopped a boat of one of the Saudi ARAMCO's contractors in *ARABIA* field area.

These two fields are located in the Saudi submerged region pursuant to the border line that separates the submerged areas between Saudi Arabia and the Islamic Republic of Iran in accordance with the agreement concluded between the two countries on 02/08/1388 AH, corresponding to 10/24/1968 AD.

The Government of Saudi Arabia is protesting this action, and demands from the Government of the Islamic Republic of Iran to ensure non-recurrence of these transgressions. Moreover, the Government of the Kingdom of Saudi Arabia reserves all rights to take whatever action it deems appropriate to protect its waters and its oil facilities. Furthermore, the Kingdom of Saudi Arabia holds the Iranian authorities fully responsible for all consequences.

The Saudi Ministry of Foreign Affairs avails itself of this opportunity to renew to the Ministry of Foreign Affairs of the Islamic Republic of Iran the assurances of its highest consideration.

---

[2] Original: Arabic. Unofficial translation provided by the Permanent Mission of the Kingdom of Saudi Arabia to the United Nations. Transmitted by letter dated 19 October 2012, from the Permanent Mission of the Kingdom of Saudi Arabia to the United Nations addressed to the Secretary-General of the United Nations.

9.   Kuwait and Saudi Arabia

Letter dated 21 November 2012 from the Permanent Representatives of Kuwait and Saudi Arabia to the United Nations addressed to the Secretary-General[10]

The Permanent Missions of Kuwait and Saudi Arabia to the United Nations present their compliments to the Secretary-General and have the honour to inform him that Iranian military vessels have carried out repeated acts of aggression and trespass into the waters of the submerged zone adjacent to the divided zone between Kuwait and Saudi Arabia (the submerged divided zone), over which those two States have exclusive sovereign rights. Most recently, three armed speed boats flying the Iranian flag crossed into the submerged Kuwaiti-Saudi zone adjacent to the divided zone at 7.30 a.m. on Friday, 24 August 2012. They stopped near drilling rig ID30 for several minutes before proceeding towards the vessel assisting the rig. Such actions could lead to confrontations endangering peace and security in the region.

It is well known that Kuwait and Saudi Arabia have exclusive sovereign rights to explore and exploit hydrocarbon resources in the Al-Durra field and the submerged divided zone.

The Governments of Kuwait and Saudi Arabia have on several occasions strongly protested and deplored those repeated acts of aggression and trespass. They demand that the Islamic Republic of Iran put an end to those actions in order to preserve their interests, respect their rights and maintain security and stability in the region.

The Governments of Kuwait and Saudi Arabia have asked the Islamic Republic of Iran for negotiations to delimit the maritime boundaries between the submerged divided zone and the waters of the Islamic Republic of Iran in accordance with international law. However, despite repeated appeals, the Governments of Kuwait and Saudi Arabia have yet to receive a response.

The Permanent Missions of Kuwait and Saudi Arabia request that the Secretary-General circulate this letter as a document of the General Assembly under agenda item 75 (a).

(Signed) Mansour Ayyad SH A Alotaibi
Permanent Representative of Kuwait to the United Nations

(Signed) Mr. Abdallah Yahya A. Al-Mouallimi
Permanent Representative of Saudi Arabia to the United Nations

---

[10] A/67/593.

IV.   OTHER INFORMATION RELEVANT TO THE LAW OF THE SEA

A.   Relevant Resolutions of the Security Council of the United Nations

Resolution 2077 (2012)

Adopted by the Security Council at its 6867th meeting, on
21 November 2012

The Security Council,

Recalling its previous resolutions concerning the situation in Somalia, especially resolutions 1814 (2008), 1816 (2008), 1838 (2008), 1844 (2008), 1846 (2008), 1851 (2008), 1897 (2009), 1918 (2010), 1950 (2010), 1976 (2011), 2015 (2011), and 2020 (2011), as well as the Statement of its President (S/PRST/2010/16) of 25 August 2010,

Continuing to be gravely concerned by the ongoing threat that piracy and armed robbery at sea against vessels pose to the prompt, safe, and effective delivery of humanitarian aid to Somalia and the region, to the safety of seafarers and other persons, to international navigation and the safety of commercial maritime routes, and to other vulnerable ships, including fishing activities in conformity with international law, and also gravely concerned by the extended range of the piracy threat into the western Indian Ocean and adjacent sea areas and the increase in pirate capacities,

Expressing concern about the reported involvement of children in piracy off the coast of Somalia,

Recognizing that the ongoing instability in Somalia contributes to the problem of piracy and armed robbery at sea off the coast of Somalia, and stressing the need for a comprehensive response by the international community to repress piracy and armed robbery at sea and tackle its underlying causes,

Recognizing the need to investigate and prosecute not only suspects captured at sea, but also anyone who incites or intentionally facilitates piracy operations, including key figures of criminal networks involved in piracy who illicitly plan, organize, facilitate, or finance and profit from such attacks, and *reiterating its concern* over persons suspected of piracy having to be released without facing justice, *reaffirming* that the failure to prosecute persons responsible for acts of piracy and armed robbery at sea off the coast of Somalia undermines anti-piracy efforts of the international community and *being determined* to create conditions to ensure that pirates are held accountable,

Reaffirming its respect for the sovereignty, territorial integrity, political independence and unity of Somalia, including Somalia's rights with respect to offshore natural resources, including fisheries, in accordance with international law, recalling the importance of preventing, in accordance with international law, illegal fishing and illegal dumping, including of toxic substances, and *stressing* the need to investigate any new allegations of such illegal fishing and dumping; *noting* the report of the Secretary-General (S/2012/783), which acknowledges difficulty in providing detailed information related to illegal, unreported, and unregulated fishing and dumping off Somalia's coast without adequate monitoring or reporting systems, and states that the United Nations has received little evidence to date to justify claims that illegal fishing and dumping are factors responsible for forcing Somali youths to resort to piracy, and that there is currently no evidence of toxic waste dumping on land and at sea; *emphasizing* that the concerns about protection of the marine environment as well as resources should not be allowed to mask the true nature of piracy off the coast of Somalia which is a transnational criminal enterprise driven primarily by the opportunity for financial gain, and *expressing appreciation* in this respect for the report of the Secretary-General on the protection of Somali natural resources and water (S/2011/661) prepared pursuant to paragraph 7 of Security Council Resolution 1976 (2011),

Further reaffirming that international law, as reflected in the United Nations Convention on the Law of the Sea of 10 December 1982 ("The Convention"), sets out the legal framework applicable to combating piracy and armed robbery at sea, as well as other ocean activities,

Underlining the primary responsibility of the Somali authorities in the fight against piracy and armed robbery at sea off the coast Somalia and *noting* the several requests from Somali authorities for international assistance to counter piracy off its coast, including the letter of 5 November 2012, from the Permanent Representative of Somalia to the United Nations expressing the appreciation of Somali authorities to the Security Council for its assistance, expressing their willingness to consider working with other States and regional organizations to combat piracy and armed robbery at sea off the coast of Somalia, and requesting that the provisions of resolution 1897 (2009) be renewed for an additional twelve months,

Commending the efforts of the European Union operation ATALANTA, North Atlantic Treaty Organization operations Allied Protector and Ocean Shield, Combined Maritime Forces' Combined Task Force 151 commanded by Denmark, New Zealand, Pakistan, Republic of Korea, Singapore, Turkey, Thailand and the United States, and other States acting in a national capacity in cooperation with Somali authorities and each other, to suppress piracy and to protect vulnerable ships transiting through the waters off the coast of Somalia, and *welcoming* the efforts of individual countries, including China, India, Japan, Malaysia, Republic of Korea, and the Russian Federation, which have deployed ships and/or aircraft in the region, as stated in the Secretary-General's report (S/2012/783),

Commending the efforts of flag States for taking appropriate measures to permit vessels sailing under their flag transiting the High Risk Area to embark vessel protection detachments and privately contracted armed security personnel, and encouraging States to regulate such activities in accordance with applicable international law and permit charters to favour arrangements that make use of such measures,

Notes the request of some Member States on the need to review the boundaries of the High Risk Area on an objective and transparent basis taking into account actual incidents of piracy, noting that the High Risk Area is set and defined by the insurance and maritime industry,

Welcoming the capacity building efforts in the region made through the International Maritime Organization (IMO) Djibouti Code of Conduct Trust Fund and the Trust Fund Supporting Initiatives of States Countering Piracy off the Coast of Somalia, as well as the European Union's planned programming under EUCAP NESTOR, and recognizing the need for all engaged international and regional organizations to cooperate fully,

Noting with appreciation the efforts made by the IMO and the shipping industry to develop and update guidance, best management practices, and recommendations to assist ships to prevent and suppress piracy attacks off the coast of Somalia, including in the Gulf of Aden, and the Indian Ocean area, and *recognizing* the work of the IMO, and the Contact Group on Piracy off the Coast of Somalia (CGPCS); in this regard, notes the efforts of the International Organization for Standardization, which has developed industry standards of training and certification for Private Maritime Security Companies when providing privately contracted armed security personnel on board ships in high-risk areas,

Noting with concern that the continuing limited capacity and domestic legislation to facilitate the custody and prosecution of suspected pirates after their capture has hindered more robust international action against the pirates off the coast of Somalia, too often has led to pirates being released without facing justice, regardless of whether there is sufficient evidence to support prosecution and *reiterating* that, consistent with the provisions of the Convention concerning the repression of piracy, the 1988 Convention for the Suppression of Unlawful Acts Against the Safety of Maritime Navigation ("SUA Convention") provides for parties to create criminal offences, establish jurisdiction, and accept delivery of persons responsible for or suspected of seizing or exercising control over a ship by force or threat thereof or any other form of intimidation,

Underlining the importance of continuing to enhance the collection, preservation and transmission to competent authorities of evidence of acts of piracy and armed robbery at sea off the coast of Somalia, and *welcoming* the ongoing work of the IMO, INTERPOL, and industry groups to develop guidance to seafarers on preservation of crime scenes following acts of piracy, and noting the importance for the successful prosecution of acts of piracy of enabling seafarers to give evidence in criminal proceedings,

Further recognizing that pirate networks continue to rely on kidnapping and hostage-taking, and that these activities help generate funding to purchase weapons, gain recruits, and continue their operational activities, thereby jeopardizing the safety and security of innocent civilians and restricting the flow of free commerce, and *welcoming* international efforts to collect and share information to disrupt the pirate enterprise, as exemplified by INTERPOL's Global Database on Maritime Piracy; and noting the ongoing initiative aimed at establishing the Regional Anti-Piracy Prosecution & Intelligence Coordination Centre, hosted by the Republic of Seychelles,

Reaffirming international condemnation of acts of kidnapping and hostage-taking, including offences contained within the International Convention against the Taking of Hostages, and *strongly condemning* the continuing practice of hostage-taking by pirates operating off the coast of Somalia, *expressing serious concern* at the inhuman conditions hostages face in captivity, *recognizing* the adverse impact on their families, *calling for* the immediate release of all hostages, and *noting* the importance of cooperation between Member States on the issue of hostage-taking and the prosecution of suspected pirates for taking hostages,

Commending the Kenya and the Seychelles' efforts to prosecute suspected pirates in their national courts, welcoming and looking forward to further engagement of Mauritius and Tanzania, and *noting* with appreciation the assistance being provided by the United Nations Office of Drugs and Crime (UNODC), the Trust Fund Supporting Initiatives of States Countering Piracy off the Coast of Somalia, and other international organizations and donors, in coordination with the CGPCS, to support Kenya, Seychelles, Somalia, and other States in the region to take steps to prosecute, or incarcerate in a third State after prosecution elsewhere, pirates, including facilitators and financiers ashore, consistent with applicable international human rights law, and emphasizing the need for States and international organizations to further enhance international efforts in this regard,

Welcoming the readiness of the national and regional administrations of Somalia to cooperate with each other and with States who have prosecuted suspected pirates with a view to enabling convicted pirates to be repatriated back to Somalia under suitable prisoner transfer arrangements, consistent with applicable international law including international human rights law,

Welcoming the report of the Secretary General (S/2012/783), as requested by resolution 2020 (2011), on the implementation of that resolution and on the situation with respect to piracy and armed robbery at sea off the coast of Somalia,

Taking note with appreciation of the reports of the Secretary-General on the modalities for the establishment of specialized Somali anti-piracy courts (S/2011/360 and S/2012/50), prepared pursuant to paragraph 26 of resolution 1976 (2011) and paragraph 16 of resolution 2015 (2011), and the ongoing efforts within the CGPCS and the United Nations Secretariat to explore possible additional mechanisms to effectively prosecute persons suspected of piracy and armed robbery at sea off the coast of Somalia, including those ashore who incite or intentionally facilitate acts of piracy,

Stressing the need for States to consider possible methods to assist the seafarers who are victims of pirates, and welcoming in this regard the ongoing work within the CGPCS and the IMO on developing guidelines for the care of seafarers and other persons who have been subjected to acts of piracy,

Recognizing the progress made by the CGPCS, UNODC, and UNPOS in the use of public information tools to raise awareness of the dangers of piracy, highlight the best practices to eradicate this criminal phenomenon, and inform the public of the dangers posed by piracy,

Further noting with appreciation the ongoing efforts by UNODC and UNDP to support efforts to enhance the capacity of the corrections system in Somalia, including regional authorities notably with the support of the Trust Fund Supporting Initiatives of States Countering Piracy off the Coast of Somalia, to incarcerate convicted pirates consistent with applicable international human rights law,

Bearing in mind the Djibouti Code of Conduct concerning the Repression of Piracy and Armed Robbery against Ships in the Western Indian Ocean and the Gulf of Aden, *noting* the operations of the newly established information sharing centres in Yemen, Kenya and Tanzania and the ongoing work regarding a regional maritime training centre in Djibouti, and *recognizing* the efforts of signatory States, including new signatory States South Africa and Mozambique, to develop the appropriate regulatory and legislative frameworks to combat piracy, enhance their capacity to patrol the waters of the region, interdict suspect vessels, and prosecute suspected pirates,

Emphasizing that peace and stability within Somalia, the strengthening of State institutions, economic and social development and respect for human rights and the rule of law are necessary to create the conditions for a durable eradication of piracy and armed robbery at sea off the coast of Somalia, and *further emphasizing* that Somalia's long-term security rests with the effective development by Somali authorities of the Somali National Security Forces,

Welcoming in this regard the election of the President on 10 September and the subsequent appointment of a Prime Minister and Cabinet, *considering* that this represents the completion of the Transition in Somalia and an important milestone in Somalia's path to more stable and accountable governance,

Noting that the joint counter-piracy efforts of the international community and private sector have resulted in a sharp decline in pirate attacks as well as hijackings since 2011 and *emphasizing* that without further action, the significant progress made in reducing the number of successful pirate attacks is reversible,

Determining that the incidents of piracy and armed robbery at sea off the coast of Somalia exacerbate the situation in Somalia, which continues to constitute a threat to international peace and security in the region,

Acting under Chapter VII of the Charter of the United Nations,

1.   *Reiterates* that it condemns and deplores all acts of piracy and armed robbery against vessels in the waters off the coast of Somalia;

2.   *Recognizes* that the ongoing instability in Somalia is one of the underlying causes of the problem of piracy and contributes to the problem of piracy and armed robbery at sea off the coast of Somalia;

3.   *Stresses* the need for a comprehensive response to repress piracy and tackle its underlying causes by the international community;

4.   *Underlines* the primary responsibility of Somali authorities in the fight against piracy and armed robbery at sea off the coast of Somalia, and requests the Somali authorities, with assistance from the Secretary-General and relevant UN entities, to pass a complete set of counter-piracy laws without further delay, and to declare an Exclusive Economic Zone in accordance with the United Nations Convention on the Law of the Sea;

5.   *Recognizes* the need to continue investigating and prosecuting all suspected pirates and *urges* States, working in conjunction with relevant international organizations, to intensify their efforts to investigate and prosecute key figures of criminal networks involved in piracy who illicitly plan, organize, facilitate, or finance and profit from such attacks;

6.   *Calling upon* the Somali authorities to interdict, and upon interdiction to investigate and prosecute pirates and to patrol the territorial waters off the coast of Somalia to suppress acts of piracy and armed robbery at sea, noting the importance of strengthening Somalia's maritime capacity, and *welcomes* support by the international community for strengthening Somalia's capacity in this regard;

7.   *Calls upon* States to cooperate also, as appropriate, on the issue of hostage taking, and the prosecution of suspected pirates for taking hostages;

8.   *Notes again* its concern regarding the findings contained in the 13 July 2012 report (S/2012/544, page 211) and resolution 2020 (2011) that escalating ransom payments and the lack of enforcement of the arms embargo established by resolution 733 (1992) are fuelling the growth of piracy off the coast of Somalia, *calls upon* all States to cooperate fully with the Somalia and Eritrea Monitoring Group including on information sharing regarding possible arms embargo violations;

9.   *Recognizes* the need for States, regional organizations, and other appropriate partners to exchange evidence and information with a view to the arrest and prosecution of key figures of criminal networks involved in piracy who illicitly plan, organize, facilitate, or finance and profit from piracy operations, and keeps under review the possibility of applying targeted sanctions against such individuals or entities if they meet the listing criteria set out in paragraph 8 resolution 1844 (2008);

10.   *Renews* its call upon States and regional organizations that have the capacity to do so, to take part in the fight against piracy and armed robbery at sea off the coast of Somalia, in particular, consistent

with this resolution and international law, by deploying naval vessels, arms and military aircraft and through seizures and disposition of boats, vessels, arms and other related equipment used in the commission of piracy and armed robbery at sea off the coast of Somalia, or for which there are reasonable grounds for suspecting such use;

11. *Commends the work* of the CGPCS to facilitate coordination in order to deter acts of piracy and armed robbery at sea off the coast of Somalia, in cooperation with the IMO, flag States, and Somali authorities and *urges* States and international organizations to continue to support these efforts;

12. *Encourages* Member States to continue to cooperate with Somali authorities in the fight against piracy and armed robbery at sea, notes the primary role of Somali authorities in the fight against piracy and armed robbery at sea off the coast of Somalia, and *decides* that for a further period of twelve months from the date of this resolution to renew the authorizations as set out in paragraph 10 of resolution 1846 (2008) and paragraph 6 of resolution 1851 (2008), as renewed by paragraph 7 of resolution 1897 (2009), paragraph 7 of resolution 1950 (2010), and paragraph 9 of resolution 2020 (2011) granted to States and regional organizations cooperating with Somali authorities in the fight against piracy and armed robbery at sea off the coast of Somalia, for which advance notification has been provided by Somali authorities to the Secretary-General;

13. *Affirms* that the authorizations renewed in this resolution apply only with respect to the situation in Somalia and shall not affect the rights or obligations or responsibilities of Member States under international law, including any rights or obligations, under the Convention, with respect to any other situation, and underscores in particular that this resolution shall not be considered as establishing customary international law; and *affirms further* that such authorizations have been renewed only following the receipt of the 5 November 2012 letter conveying the consent of Somali authorities;

14. *Further affirms* that the measures imposed by paragraph 5 of resolution 733 (1992) and further elaborated upon by paragraphs 1 and 2 of resolution 1425 (2002) do not apply to weapons and military equipment destined for the sole use of Member States and regional organizations undertaking measures in accordance with paragraph 9 above or to supplies of technical assistance to Somalia solely for the purposes set out in paragraph 6 of resolution 1950 (2010) which have been exempted from those measures in accordance with the procedure set out in paragraphs 11 (b) and 12 of resolution 1772 (2007);

15. *Requests* that cooperating States take appropriate steps to ensure that the activities they undertake pursuant to the authorizations in paragraph 9 do not have the practical effect of denying or impairing the right of innocent passage to the ships of any third State;

16. *Calls on* the Somali authorities to make all efforts to bring to justice those who are using Somali territory to plan, facilitate, or undertake criminal acts of piracy and armed robbery at sea and *calls upon* Member States to assist Somalia, at the request of Somali authorities and with notification to the Secretary-General, to strengthen capacity in Somalia, including regional authorities, and *stresses* that any measures undertaken pursuant to this paragraph shall be consistent with applicable international human rights law;

17. *Calls upon* all States, and in particular flag, port, and coastal States, States of the nationality of victims, and perpetrators of piracy and armed robbery, and other States with relevant jurisdiction under international law and national legislation, to cooperate in determining jurisdiction, and in the investigation and prosecution of all persons responsible for acts of piracy and armed robbery off the coast of Somalia, including anyone who incites or facilitates an act of piracy, consistent with applicable international law including international human rights law to ensure that all pirates handed over to judicial authorities are subject to a judicial process, and to render assistance by, among other actions, providing disposition and logistics assistance with respect to persons under their jurisdiction and control, such as victims and witnesses and persons detained as a result of operations conducted under this resolution;

18. *Calls upon* all States to criminalize piracy under their domestic law and to favourably consider the prosecution of suspected, and imprisonment of convicted, pirates apprehended off the coast of Somalia, and their facilitators and financiers ashore, consistent with applicable international law including international human rights law;

19.   *Reiterates* its decision to continue its consideration, as a matter of urgency, of the establishment of specialized anti-piracy courts in Somalia and other States in the region with substantial international participation and/or support, as set forth in resolution 2015 (2011), and the importance of such courts having jurisdiction over not only suspects captured at sea, but also anyone who incites or intentionally facilitates piracy operations, including key figures of criminal networks involved in piracy who illicitly plan, organize, facilitate, or finance and profit from such attacks, and *emphasizes* the need for strengthened cooperation of States, regional, and international organizations in holding such individuals accountable, and encourages the CGPCS to continue its discussions in this regard;

20.   *Welcomes*, in this context, that the report of the Secretary-General pursuant to resolution 2015 (2011) contains detailed implementation proposals on ways to ensure that suspected pirates are held accountable through the due process of law in accordance with international standards, and encourages action in this field at the federal level in Somalia;

21.   *Urges* all States to take appropriate actions under their existing domestic law to prevent the illicit financing of acts of piracy and the laundering of its proceeds;

22.   *Urges* States, in cooperation with INTERPOL and Europol, to further investigate international criminal networks involved in piracy off the coast of Somalia, including those responsible for illicit financing and facilitation;

23.   *Commends* INTERPOL for the creation of a global piracy database designed to consolidate information about piracy off the coast of Somalia and facilitate the development of actionable analysis for law enforcement, and *urges* all States to share such information with INTERPOL for use in the database, through appropriate channels;

24.   *Stresses* in this context the need to support the investigation and prosecution of those who illicitly finance, plan, organize, or unlawfully profit from pirate attacks off the coast of Somalia;

25.   *Urges* States and international organizations to share evidence and information for anti-piracy law enforcement purposes with a view to ensuring effective prosecution of suspected, and imprisonment of convicted, pirates;

26.   *Commends* the establishment of the Trust Fund Supporting the Initiatives of States Countering Piracy off the Coast of Somalia and the IMO Djibouti Code Trust Fund and *urges* both state and non-state actors affected by piracy, most notably the international shipping community, to contribute to them;

27.   *Urges* States parties to the Convention and the SUA Convention to implement fully their relevant obligations under these Conventions and customary international law and cooperate with the UNODC, IMO, and other States and other international organizations to build judicial capacity for the successful prosecution of persons suspected of piracy and armed robbery at sea off the coast of Somalia;

28.   *Urges* States individually or within the framework of competent international organizations to positively consider investigating any new allegations of illegal fishing and illegal dumping, including of toxic substances, with a view to prosecuting such offences when committed by persons under their jurisdiction; *encourages* increased efforts to monitor and report on such allegations; *takes note* of the report of the Secretary-General (S/2012/783), which acknowledges difficulty in providing detailed information related to illegal, unreported, and unregulated fishing and dumping off Somalia's coast without adequate monitoring or reporting systems, and states that the United Nations has received little evidence to date to justify claims that illegal fishing and dumping are factors responsible for forcing Somali youths to resort to piracy, and that there is currently no evidence of toxic waste dumping on land and at sea; and *emphasizes* that the concerns about protection of the marine environment as well as resources should not be allowed to mask the true nature of piracy off the coast of Somalia which is a transnational criminal enterprise driven primarily by the opportunity for financial gain; and *takes note* of the Secretary-General's intention to include updates on these issues in his reports relating to piracy off the Coast of Somalia;

29.   *Welcomes* the recommendations and guidance of the IMO on preventing and suppressing piracy and armed robbery against ships, *underlines* the importance of implementing such recommendations and guidance by all stakeholders, particularly the shipping industry, and of flag States ensuring, as appropriate, the implementation of such recommendations and guidance, and *urges* States, in collaboration

with the shipping and insurance industries, and the IMO, to continue to develop and implement avoidance, evasion, and defensive best practices and advisories to take when under attack or when sailing in the waters off the coast of Somalia, and further urges States to make their citizens and vessels available for forensic investigation as appropriate at the first suitable port of call immediately following an act or attempted act of piracy or armed robbery at sea or release from captivity;

30.   *Encourages* flag States and port States to further consider the development of safety and security measures onboard vessels, including, where applicable, developing regulations for the deployment of PCASP on board ships through a consultative process, including through the IMO and ISO;

31.   *Invites* the IMO to continue its contributions to the prevention and suppression of acts of piracy and armed robbery against ships in coordination, in particular, with the UNODC, the World Food Program (WFP), the shipping industry, and all other parties concerned, and *recognizes* the IMO's role concerning privately contracted armed security personnel on board ships in high-risk areas;

32.   *Notes* the importance of securing the safe delivery of WFP assistance by sea, welcomes the ongoing work by the WFP, EU operation ATALANTA and flag States with regard to Vessel Protection Detachments on WFP vessels;

33.   *Requests* States and regional organizations cooperating with Somali authorities to inform the Security Council and the Secretary-General in nine months of the progress of actions undertaken in the exercise of the authorizations provided in paragraph 9 above and further requests all States contributing through the CGPCS to the fight against piracy off the coast of Somalia, including Somalia and other States in the region, to report by the same deadline on their efforts to establish jurisdiction and cooperation in the investigation and prosecution of piracy;

34.   *Requests* the Secretary-General to report to the Security Council within 11 months of the adoption of this resolution on the implementation of this resolution and on the situation with respect to piracy and armed robbery at sea off the coast of Somalia;

35.   *Expresses* its intention to review the situation and consider, as appropriate, renewing the authorizations provided in paragraph 9 above for additional periods upon the request of Somali authorities;

36.   *Decides* to remain seized of the matter.

B.   Relevant Resolutions from Intergovernmental Organizations

AALCO: Resolution on Half-Day Special Meeting on "The Law of the Sea Responses to Piracy:
International Legal Challenges", 22 June 2012[1]
(Deliberated)

The Asian-African Legal Consultative Organization at its Fifty-First Session,

Considering the Secretariat Document No. AALCO/51/ABUJA/ 2012/S 2;

Noting with appreciation the introductory remarks of the Deputy Secretary-General and the views expressed by the Chairperson and the Panelists and the statements of the Member States during the Special Meeting on "The Law of the Sea – Responses to Piracy: International Legal Challenges" jointly organized by the Government of the Federal Republic of Nigeria, AALCO and the **United Nations Division of Ocean Affairs and the Law of the Sea** held on 20th June 2012 at Abuja, Nigeria

Recognizing the universal character of the United Nations Convention on the Law of the Sea 1982 (UNCLOS), and its legal framework governing the issues relating to the management of the oceans;

Mindful of the historical contribution made by the Asian-African Legal Consultative Organization in the elaboration of the UNCLOS;

Conscious that the AALCO has been regularly following the implementation of the UNCLOS and its implementing agreements;

Hopeful that in view of the importance of the law of the sea issues, AALCO would maintain its consideration on the agenda item and continue to perform its historical role on the law of the sea matters;

Taking note of the deliberations at the United Nations Open-ended Informal Consultative Process established by the United Nations General Assembly to facilitate annual review of the developments in ocean affairs;

Welcoming the pre-eminent contribution and active role being played by the institutions established under the UNCLOS in relation to the peaceful settlement of disputes with regard to ocean related matters, the establishment of the outer limits of the Continental Shelf and the administration of the "Area";

Noting with satisfaction the upcoming commemoration of the 30th Anniversary of the opening for signature of UNCLOS on 10 December 2012;

Being aware of the challenges faced by the international community on account of piracy:

Condemning the increasing incidents of all acts of piracy and armed robbery against vessels;

1.   **Reaffirms** that in accordance with the UNCLOS, the "Area" and its resources are the common heritage of mankind.

2.   **Encourages** the full and effective participation of its Member States in the work of the International Seabed Authority, and other related bodies established by the United Nations Convention on the Law of the Sea, as well as in the United Nations Informal Consultative Process and also through effective contribution to the work of the Commission on the Limits of Continental Shelf, so as to ensure and safeguard their legitimate interests.

3.   **Calls upon** the Member States that have not yet done so to ratify or accede to and implement fully the 1982 United Nations Convention on the Law of the Sea.

4.   **Requests** the Secretary-General to forward this resolution to the Secretariat of UNCLOS in commemoration of the 30th Anniversary of the UNCLOS.

---

[1] AALCO/RES/51/SP 2.

5.   **Also Requests** the Secretary-General to explore the possibility of bringing out a comprehensive study on anti-piracy legislations in order to assist the Member States on the subject matter.

6.   **Decides** to place this item on the provisional agenda of the Fifty-Second Annual Session.

C.   Recent Judgments, Awards, and Orders

International Court of Justice:
Territorial and Maritime Dispute (Nicaragua v. Colombia)
Judgment delivered on 19 November 2012[2]

The Court finds that Colombia has sovereignty over the maritime features in dispute and draws a single maritime boundary

THE HAGUE, 19 November 2012. The International Court of Justice (ICJ), the principal judicial organ of the United Nations, has today rendered its Judgment in the case concerning the Territorial and Maritime Dispute (Nicaragua v. Colombia).

In its Judgment, which is final, without appeal and binding on the Parties, the Court,

(1) finds, unanimously, that the Republic of Colombia has sovereignty over the islands at Alburquerque, Bajo Nuevo, East-Southeast Cays, Quitasueño, Roncador, Serrana and Serranilla;

(2) finds, by fourteen votes to one, admissible the Republic of Nicaragua's claim contained in its final submission I (3) requesting the Court to adjudge and declare that "[t]he appropriate form of delimitation, within the geographical and legal framework constituted by the mainland coasts of Nicaragua and Colombia, is a continental shelf boundary dividing by equal parts the overlapping entitlements to a continental shelf of both Parties";

(3) finds, unanimously, that it cannot uphold the Republic of Nicaragua's claim contained in its final submission I (3);

(4) decides, unanimously, that the line of the single maritime boundary delimiting the continental shelf and the exclusive economic zones of the Republic of Nicaragua and the Republic of Colombia shall follow geodetic lines connecting the points with co-ordinates:

Latitude north	Longitude west
1. 13° 46' 35.7"	81° 29' 34.7"
2. 13° 31' 08.0"	81° 45' 59.4"
3. 13° 03' 15.8"	81° 46' 22.7"
4. 12° 50' 12.8"	81° 59' 22.6"
5. 12° 07' 28.8"	82° 07' 27.7"
6. 12° 00' 04.5"	81° 57' 57.8"

From point 1, the maritime boundary line shall continue due east along the parallel of latitude (co-ordinates 13° 46' 35.7" N) until it reaches the 200-nautical-mile limit from the baselines from which the breadth of the territorial sea of Nicaragua is measured. From point 6 (with co-ordinates 12° 00' 04.5" N and 81° 57' 57.8" W), located on a 12-nautical-mile envelope of arcs around Alburquerque, the maritime boundary line shall continue along that envelope of arcs until it reaches point 7 (with co-ordinates 12° 11' 53.5" N and 81° 38' 16.6" W) which is located on the parallel passing through the southernmost point on the 12-nautical-mile envelope of arcs around East-Southeast Cays. The boundary line then follows that parallel until it reaches the southernmost point of the 12-nautical-mile envelope of arcs around East-Southeast Cays at point 8 (with co-ordinates 12° 11' 53.5" N and 81° 28' 29.5" W) and continues along that envelope of arcs until its most eastward point (point 9 with co-ordinates 12° 24' 09.3" N and 81° 14' 43.9" W). From that point the boundary line follows the parallel of latitude (co-ordinates 12° 24' 09.3" N) until it reaches the 200–nautical–mile limit from the baselines from which the territorial sea of Nicaragua is measured;

(5) decides, unanimously, that the single maritime boundary around Quitasueño and Serrana shall follow, respectively, a 12-nautical-mile envelope of arcs measured from QS 32 and from low-tide elevations located within

---

[2] Source: ICJ/Press Release No. 2012/33 of 19 November 2012.

12 nautical miles from QS 32, and a 12-nautical-mile envelope of arcs measured from Serrana Cay and the other cays in its vicinity;

(6) rejects, unanimously, the Republic of Nicaragua's claim contained in its final submissions requesting the Court to declare that the Republic of Colombia is not acting in accordance with its obligations under international law by preventing the Republic of Nicaragua from having access to natural resources to the east of the 82nd meridian.

———————

1. Sovereignty

The Court recalls that the dispute between the Parties concerns sovereignty over maritime features located in the Caribbean Sea, namely, the Alburquerque Cays, East-Southeast Cays, Roncador, Serrana, Quitasueño, Serranilla and Bajo Nuevo. All these remain above water at high tide and thus, as islands, they are capable of appropriation. However, as to Quitasueño, the Court finds that it comprises only one tiny island, referred to as QS 32, and a number of low-tide elevations (features which are above water at low tide but submerged at high tide).

The Court then notes that, under the terms of the 1928 Treaty concerning Territorial Questions at Issue between Colombia and Nicaragua, Colombia has sovereignty not only over San Andrés, Providencia and Santa Catalina, but also over the other islands, islets and reefs "forming part" of the San Andrés Archipelago. Thus, in order to determine sovereignty, the Court must first ascertain what constitutes the San Andrés Archipelago. The Court, however, concludes that neither the 1928 Treaty nor the historical records is conclusive as to the composition of that Archipelago.

The Court therefore proceeds to examine arguments and evidence which are not based on the composition of the Archipelago under the 1928 Treaty. The Court finds that neither Nicaragua nor Colombia has established that it had title to the disputed maritime features by virtue of uti possidetis juris (a principle according to which, upon independence, new States inherit territories and boundaries of former colonial provinces), because nothing clearly indicates whether these features were attributed to the colonial provinces of Nicaragua or of Colombia. The Court therefore turns to the question whether sovereignty can be established on the basis of a State's acts manifesting a display of authority on a given territory (effectivités). The Court finds that for many decades Colombia continuously and consistently acted à titre de souverain in respect of the maritime features in dispute. This exercise of sovereign authority was public and there is no evidence that it met with any protest from Nicaragua prior to 1969, when the dispute crystallized. Moreover, the evidence of Colombia's acts of administration with respect to the islands is in contrast to the absence of any evidence of acts à titre de souverain on the part of Nicaragua. The facts thus provide very strong support for Colombia's claim of sovereignty over the maritime features in dispute. The Court also notes that, while not being evidence of sovereignty, Nicaragua's conduct with regard to the maritime features in dispute, the practice of third States and maps afford some support to Colombia's claim.

The Court concludes that Colombia, and not Nicaragua, has sovereignty over the islands at Alburquerque, Bajo Nuevo, East-Southeast Cays, Quitasueño, Roncador, Serrana and Serranilla.

2. Admissibility of Nicaragua's claim for delimitation of a continental shelf extending beyond 200 nautical miles

The Court notes that in its Application and Memorial, Nicaragua requested the Court to determine the "single maritime boundary" between the continental shelf areas and exclusive economic zones appertaining respectively to Nicaragua and Colombia in the form of a median line between the mainland coasts of the two States. In its Reply and in its final submission I (3) Nicaragua requested the Court to effect a continental shelf boundary dividing by equal parts the overlapping entitlements of the Parties - extended continental shelf of Nicaragua beyond 200 nautical miles and 200-nautical-mile continental shelf of Colombia. This is a new claim, but this fact does not, in itself, render the claim inadmissible. This claim still concerns the delimitation of the continental shelf, arises directly out of the Parties' dispute and does not transform its subject-matter. The Court concludes that the claim contained in final submission I (3) by Nicaragua is admissible.

3. Consideration of Nicaragua's claim for delimitation of a continental shelf extending beyond 200 nautical miles

The Court observes that, in its recent jurisprudence, it has stated that "any claim of continental shelf rights beyond 200 miles [by a State party to the 1982 United Nations Convention on the Law of the Sea (UNCLOS)] must be in accordance with Article 76 of UNCLOS and reviewed by the Commission on the Limits of the Continental Shelf". Given the object and purpose of UNCLOS, as stipulated in its Preamble, the fact that Colombia is not a party thereto does not relieve Nicaragua of its obligations under Article 76. The Court notes that Nicaragua submitted to the Commission only "Preliminary Information" which, by its own admission, falls short of meeting the requirements for the Commission to be able to make a recommendation. As the Court was not presented with any further information, it finds that, in the present proceedings, Nicaragua has not established that it has a continental margin that extends far enough to overlap with Colombia's 200-nautical-mile entitlement to the continental shelf, measured from Colombia's mainland coast. The Court thus is not in a position to delimit the boundary between an extended continental shelf of Nicaragua and Colombia's continental shelf. The Court concludes that Nicaragua's claim contained in its final submission I (3) cannot be upheld.

4. Maritime boundary

The Court notes that notwithstanding its decision regarding Nicaragua's final submission I (3), it is still called upon to effect a delimitation between the overlapping maritime entitlements of Colombia and Nicaragua within 200 nautical miles of the Nicaraguan coast.

The Court begins by determining what the relevant coasts of the Parties are, namely, those coasts the projections of which overlap. For Nicaragua, the relevant coast is its whole coast with the exception of the short stretch of coast near Punta de Perlas. For Colombia, the relevant coast is the entire coastline of its islands, except Quitasueño, Serranilla and Bajo Nuevo. The Court then considers the extent of the relevant maritime area in which the potential entitlements of the Parties overlap. This area extends 200 nautical miles eastwards from the Nicaraguan coast. In the north and south, the limits of the relevant area were determined in such a way so as not to encroach upon any existing boundaries or interests of third States (see sketch-map No. 7: The relevant maritime area as identified by the Court).

To effect the delimitation, the Court follows the three-stage methodology employed in its case law.

First, the Court selects base points and constructs a provisional median line between the Nicaraguan coast and the western coasts of the relevant Colombian islands, which are opposite to the Nicaraguan coast (see sketch-map No. 8: Construction of the provisional median line).

Secondly, the Court examines the relevant circumstances which may require an adjustment or shifting of the provisional median line to produce an equitable result. It notes that the substantial disparity between the relevant Colombian coast and that of Nicaragua (1:8.2), as well as the need to avoid any cut-off effect of the delimitation line vis-à-vis the Parties' coastal projections, are such circumstances. The Court further notes that, while legitimate security concerns will be borne in mind in determining whether the provisional median line should be adjusted or shifted, the conduct of the Parties, issues of access to natural resources and delimitations already effected in the area are not relevant circumstances in the present case.

Having thus identified the relevant circumstances applicable in the present case, the Court proceeds by way of shifting the provisional median line. In this context, the Court draws a distinction between that part of the relevant area which lies between the Nicaraguan mainland and the western coasts of Alburquerque Cays, San Andrés, Providencia and Santa Catalina, where the relationship is one of opposite coasts, and the part which lies to the east of those islands, where the relationship is more complex. In the first western part of the relevant area, the relevant circumstances call for the provisional median line to be shifted eastwards. For this purpose, the base points located on the Nicaraguan and Colombian islands, respectively, should have different weights, namely, a weighting of one to each of the Colombian base points and a weighting of three to each of the Nicaraguan base points. The weighted line, constructed on this basis, has a curved shape with a large number of turning points (see sketch-map No. 9: Construction of the weighted line). The Court therefore reduces the number of turning points and connects them by geodetic lines (see sketch-map No. 10: The simplified weighted line).

The Court considers, however, that to extend that line further north and south would not lead to an equitable result because it would still leave Colombia with a significantly larger share of the relevant area than that accorded to Nicaragua, notwithstanding the fact that Nicaragua's relevant coast is more than eight times the length of

Colombia's relevant coast; and it would cut off Nicaragua from the areas east of the principal Colombian islands into which the Nicaraguan coast projects.

The Court considers that an equitable result is achieved by continuing the boundary line along the parallels of latitude to 200 nautical miles from the Nicaraguan coast. In the north, this line follows the parallel passing through the northernmost point of the 12-nautical-mile territorial sea of Roncador. In the south, the maritime boundary will first follow the 12–nautical–mile territorial sea of Alburquerque Cays and East-Southeast Cays and then, from the most eastward point of the latter's territorial sea, the parallel of latitude. As Quitasueño and Serrana would consequently be left on the Nicaraguan side of the boundary line, the line of the maritime boundary around each of these features follows the 12-nautical-mile territorial sea around them (see sketch-map No. 11: Course of the maritime boundary).

Thirdly, the Court notes that the boundary line has the effect of dividing the relevant area between the Parties in a ratio of approximately 1:3.44 in Nicaragua's favour, while the ratio of relevant coasts is approximately 1:8.2. The question therefore is whether, in the circumstances of the present case, this disproportion is so great as to render the result inequitable. The Court concludes that, taking account of all the circumstances of the present case, the result achieved by the maritime delimitation does not entail such a disproportionality as to create an inequitable result.

5. Nicaragua's request for a declaration

In addition to its claims regarding a maritime boundary, in its final submissions, Nicaragua requested that the Court adjudge and declare that "Colombia is not acting in accordance with her obligations under international law by stopping and otherwise hindering Nicaragua from accessing and disposing of her natural resources to the east of the 82nd meridian".

The Court observes that Nicaragua's request for this declaration is made in the context of proceedings regarding a maritime boundary which had not been settled prior to the decision of the Court. The consequence of the Court's Judgment is that the maritime boundary between Nicaragua and Colombia throughout the relevant area has now been delimited as between the Parties. In this regard, the Court observes that the Judgment attributes to Colombia part of the maritime spaces in respect of which Nicaragua seeks a declaration regarding access to natural resources. In this context, the Court considers that Nicaragua's claim is unfounded.

Composition of the Court

The Court was composed as follows: President Tomka; Vice-President Sepúlveda-Amor; Judges Owada, Abraham, Keith, Bennouna, Skotnikov, Cançado Trindade, Yusuf, Greenwood, Xue, Donoghue, Sebutinde; Judges ad hoc Mensah, Cot; Registrar Couvreur.

Judge OWADA appends a dissenting opinion to the Judgment of the Court; Judge ABRAHAM appends a separate opinion to the Judgment of the Court; Judges KEITH and XUE append declarations to the Judgment of the Court; Judge DONOGHUE appends a separate opinion to the Judgment of the Court; Judges ad hoc MENSAH and COT append declarations to the Judgment of the Court.

*

A summary of the Judgment appears in the document "Summary No. 2012/5". This press release, the summary, and the full text of the Judgment can be found on the Court's website (www.icj-cij.org), under the heading "Cases".

_____

Note: The Court's press releases do not constitute official documents.

_____

The International Court of Justice (ICJ) is the principal judicial organ of the United Nations. It was established by the United Nations Charter in June 1945 and began its activities in April 1946. The seat of the Court is at the Peace Palace in The Hague (Netherlands). Of the six principal organs of the United Nations, it is the only one not located in New York. The Court has a twofold role: first, to settle, in accordance with international law, legal disputes submitted to it by States (its judgments have binding force and are without appeal for the parties concerned); and, second, to give advisory opinions on legal questions referred to it by duly authorized United Nations organs and agencies of the system. The Court is composed of 15 judges elected for a nine-year term by the General Assembly and the Security Council of the United Nations. Independent of the United Nations Secretariat, it is assisted by a Registry, its own international secretariat, whose activities are both judicial and diplomatic, as well as administrative. The official languages of the Court are French and English. Also known as the "World Court", it is the only court of a universal character with general jurisdiction.

The ICJ, a court open only to States for contentious proceedings, and to certain organs and institutions of the United Nations system for advisory proceedings, should not be confused with the other - mostly criminal ☐ judicial institutions based in The Hague and adjacent areas, such as the International Criminal Tribunal for the former Yugoslavia (ICTY, an ad hoc court created by the Security Council), the International Criminal Court (ICC, the first permanent international criminal court, established by treaty, which does not belong to the United Nations system), the Special Tribunal for Lebanon (STL, an independent judicial body composed of Lebanese and international judges, which is not a United Nations tribunal and does not form part of the Lebanese judicial system), or the Permanent Court of Arbitration (PCA, an independent institution which assists in the establishment of arbitral tribunals and facilitates their work, in accordance with the Hague Convention of 1899).

———————

Information Department:

Mr. Andrey Poskakukhin, First Secretary of the Court, Head of Department (+31 (0)70 302 2336)
Mr. Boris Heim, Information Officer (+31 (0)70 302 2337)
Ms Joanne Moore, Associate Information Officer (+31 (0)70 302 2394)
Ms Genoveva Madurga, Administrative Assistant (+31 (0)70 302 2396)

Annex to Press Release 2012/33

–   Sketch-map No. 7: The relevant maritime area as identified by the Court;[3]

–   Sketch-map No. 8: Construction of the provisional median line;[3]

–   Sketch-map No. 9: Construction of the weighted line;[3]

–   Sketch-map No. 10: The simplified weighted line;[3]

–   Sketch-map No. 11: Course of the maritime boundary.

---

[3] Note by the Editor: This map can be found at http://www.icj-cij.org/docket/files/124/17162.pdf.

Sketch-map No. 11: Course of the Maritime Boundary

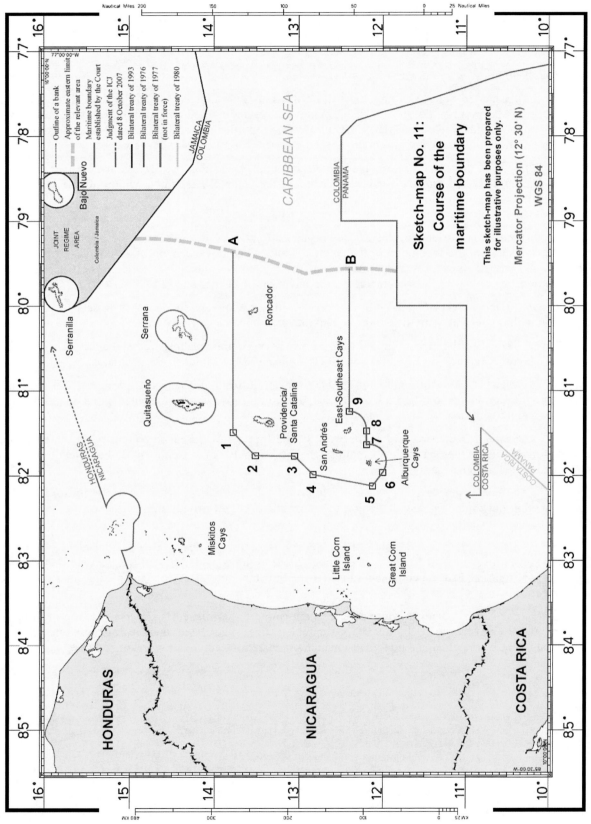

D.   Other Documents

Declaration on the Thirtieth Anniversary of the Opening for Signature
of the 1982 United Nations Convention on the Law of the Sea[4]

The Meeting of States Parties,

Recalling that the States that negotiated the United Nations Convention on the Law of the Sea were prompted by the desire to settle, in a spirit of mutual understanding and cooperation, all issues relating to the law of the sea and by their awareness of the historic significance of the Convention as an important contribution to the maintenance of peace, justice and progress for all peoples of the world,

Recalling also the crucial role played by Ambassador Arvid Pardo of Malta and, in particular, his visionary speech delivered on 1 November 1967 before the General Assembly, leading to the adoption of the Convention,

Recognizing the pre-eminent contribution provided by the Convention to the strengthening of peace, security, cooperation and friendly relations among all nations in conformity with the principles of justice and equal rights and to the promotion of the economic and social advancement of all peoples of the world, in accordance with the purposes and principles of the United Nations as set forth in the Charter of the United Nations, as well as to the sustainable development of the oceans and seas,

Recalling the universal and unified character of the Convention and that it sets out the legal framework within which all activities in the oceans and seas must be carried out,

1.   *Welcomes* the upcoming thirtieth anniversary of the opening for signature of the United Nations Convention on the Law of the Sea on 10 December 1982 at Montego Bay, Jamaica;

2.   *Pays tribute* to the negotiators of the Convention from all States that participated in the Third United Nations Conference on the Law of the Sea, and to all those who contributed to its adoption, entry into force, and universality;

3.   *Commends* the progress in the work of the International Seabed Authority, the International Tribunal for the Law of the Sea and the Commission on the Limits of the Continental Shelf, the three organs established by the Convention;

4.   *Welcomes* the decision of the Assembly of the International Seabed Authority to convene a special meeting during its eighteenth session to commemorate the thirtieth anniversary of the opening for signature of the Convention;

5.   *Also welcomes* the decision of the General Assembly to devote two days of plenary meetings at its sixty-seventh session, on 10 and 11 December 2012, to the consideration of the item entitled "Oceans and the law of the sea" and the commemoration of the thirtieth anniversary of the opening for signature of the Convention;[5]

6.   *Further welcomes* the activities to commemorate the thirtieth anniversary of the opening for signature of the Convention by the Secretary-General, States, specialized agencies of the United Nations system and intergovernmental and non-governmental organizations and other relevant bodies;

---

[4] SPLOS/249.

[5] Resolution 66/231, para. 245.

7.   *Invites* States Parties to make contributions to the established trust funds related to the law of the sea,[6] and encourages continued capacity-building initiatives in support of the implementation of the Convention;

8.   *Expresses its appreciation* to the Secretary-General for his annual reports on oceans and the law of the sea and for the high standard of the support provided by the Division for Ocean Affairs and the Law of the Sea to the work of the Meeting of States Parties and the Commission on the Limits of the Continental Shelf;

9.   *Calls upon* States that have not yet done so to become parties to the Convention and the Agreement relating to the Implementation of Part XI of the United Nations Convention on the Law of the Sea of 10 December 1982.

---

[6] Voluntary Trust Fund for the purpose of facilitating the preparation of submissions to the Commission on the Limits of the Continental Shelf for developing States, in particular the least developed countries and small island developing States, in compliance with article 76 of the United Nations Convention on the Law of the Sea (fund code: KUA); Voluntary Trust Fund for the purpose of defraying the cost of participation of the members of the Commission on the Limits of the Continental Shelf from developing States in the meetings of the Commission (fund code: KJA); Hamilton Shirley Amerasinghe Memorial Fellowship on the Law of the Sea (fund code: TLA/Project No. 9681); Voluntary Trust Fund to assist States in the settlement of disputes through the International Tribunal for the Law of the Sea (fund code: KFA); International Seabed Authority Endowment Fund; and International Seabed Authority Voluntary Trust Fund.